HOW TO PLAY
THEOLOGICAL PING-PONG

And Other Essays on
Faith and Reason

HOW TO PLAY THEOLOGICAL PING-PONG

And Other Essays on Faith and Reason

Basil Mitchell

Edited by
William J. Abraham
and
Robert W. Prevost

Hodder & Stoughton

LONDON SYDNEY AUCKLAND TORONTO

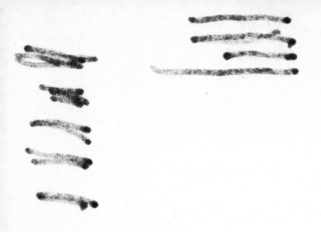

British Library Cataloguing in Publication Data
Mitchell, Basil, *1917–*
 How to play theological ping pong.
 1. Christian life. Faith
 I. Title II. Abraham, William J. (William James), *1947–*
 III. Prevost, Robert W. IV. Series
 248.4

 ISBN 0-340-51383-7

First published in Great Britain 1990

Published by Hodder and Stoughton,
a division of Hodder and Stoughton Ltd,
Mill Road, Dunton Green, Sevenoaks, Kent TN13 2YA
Editorial Office: 47 Bedford Square, London WC1B 3DP

Photoset by Rowland Phototypesetting Ltd
Bury St Edmunds, Suffolk

Printed in Great Britain by
Richard Clay Ltd, Bungay, Suffolk

CONTENTS

EDITORS' PREFACE

Our editorial responsibilities in the production of this volume have been minimal. We made the selection of papers to be included, decided on the order, and prepared the manuscript for presentation to the publishers. The content belongs entirely to Basil Mitchell. For us the work has been a labour of affection which represents a debt of gratitude to an esteemed teacher that can never be adequately repaid. We are very grateful to Mary Ann Marshall of Perkins School of Theology, Southern Methodist University, for her splendid work in typing, and to David Wavre of Hodder & Stoughton for his timely advice. We are also grateful to Dr Andrew Walker, Director of the C. S. Lewis Centre, for his enthusiasm and encouragement.

Basil Mitchell has had a distinguished career as a scholar and teacher at the University of Oxford. For twenty years he was Fellow and Tutor in Philosophy at Keble College. From there he moved to Oriel College, where he was Nolloth Professor of the Philosophy of the Christian Religion from 1968 until 1984. He has made a deeply significant contribution to philosophy as well as serving on Church of England Working Parties on Ethical Questions from 1964 until 1978 and on the Church of England Doctrine Commission from 1978 until 1984. His writings are a model of lucidity and fair-mindedness.

The essays published here were written for a variety of occasions. Some were read at academic conferences; others were read to various religious groups and societies. Two of them ('The Layman's Predicament' and 'How to Play Theological Ping-Pong') were originally given at an informal group of lay and clerical members of Oxford University, at which it was customary for a serious theme to be lightly treated. They appear here as originally presented.

As is almost inevitable in a collection of this kind, there are occasional overlaps between papers which we could have avoided only by infelicitous cuttings or by omitting a paper otherwise worthy of inclusion.

The problem of 'gender-specific language' is one that we have also had to consider. On stylistic grounds we have decided not to attempt to follow the now common practice of a strenuous avoidance of gender-specific language. Instead, we have chosen to retain, in all but a few instances, Basil Mitchell's customary generic usage of 'man' and 'he'.

We are especially happy to see this collection of Basil Mitchell's papers published under the auspices of the C. S. Lewis Centre. They represent an unusually sensitive commentary on some crucial issues of vital interest both to the academy and to thoughtful Christians everywhere. They are written in a style which is accessible to the lay person, yet they deal with topics of fundamental significance for those interested in the relation between Christianity and the life of the mind.

We hope that those who encounter Basil Mitchell for the first time in these essays will be inspired and provoked to explore the rich fare which he has provided elsewhere in his writings.

William J. Abraham
Robert W. Prevost

ACKNOWLEDGEMENTS

Acknowledgements for permission to reprint the papers in this collection are gratefully made to the following:

For 'Contemporary Challenges to Christian Apologetics', *Journal of the Irish Christian Study Centre*, forthcoming, to the Editors of the *Journal of the Irish Christian Study Centre*;

For 'Should the Law be Christian?', *The Month*, March 1987, pp. 95–9, to the Editors of *The Month*;

For '"Indoctrination"', © Basil Mitchell, from *The Fourth R, the Durham Report on Religious Education* (London: SPCK, 1970), pp. 353–8, to SPCK and to the author;

For 'Reason and Commitment in the Academic Vocation', *Oxford Review of Education* 2 (1976), pp. 101–9, to the Carfax Publishing Company and to the author;

For *Neutrality and Commitment* (Oxford: Oxford University Press, 1968), to Oxford University Press;

For 'Faith and Reason: A False Antithesis?', *Religious Studies* 16 (1980), pp. 131–44, to Cambridge University Press;

For 'Philosophy and Theology', © Basil Mitchell, from Gerard J. Hughes (ed.), *The Philosophical Assessment of Theology: Essays in Honour of Frederick C. Copleston* (Tunbridge Wells: Search Press and Georgetown University Press, 1987), pp. 3–14, to the publishers and to the author.

A full reference to the original provenance of each paper in this collection is given in a footnote to its title.

1

THE LAYMAN'S PREDICAMENT*

Ian Kennedy, Professor of Law at King's College, London, recently ran a television series on problems of medical ethics. One of these began with a Hospital Ethics Committee in session. Among the assembled doctors and nurses was a single clergyman, the hospital chaplain, conspicuous in his dog collar. After showing us a period of discussion on the committee (in which I thought the chaplain showed up very well) the programme shifted to Ian Kennedy and a panel of doctors, some of whom were members of the committee. 'I was interested to observe,' said Kennedy in his slightly portentous manner, 'that you had only one layman on your committee.'

It is in this sense that I use the word 'layman' in my title, the sense in which we are all laymen in relation to experts, having no alternative but to defer to them in whatever concerns their expertise. At first mention this situation causes no particular anxiety. Experts are specialised people, each occupying a small territory, which one only rarely has occasion to enter. Elsewhere are wide expanses where one is free to roam at will. But it takes only a moment to reflect that every part of that wide expanse is also the domain of some expert, most probably of a multiplicity of experts. Enclosure has been going on for centuries and there is no longer any common land. And it is this which constitutes the layman's predicament. He needs to make up his mind about innumerable issues, and yet he knows that he cannot conceivably muster the resources that are required to make a reasonable judgement.

* Originally read to 'Theological Wine', an informal theological group in Oxford, 1983.

The problem arises at a variety of levels. What I particularly have in mind is the predicament of the individual – any individual – in relation to the things that matter most to him, his political and religious convictions, for example. These are the things it is most important to get right, and at the same time they are the most difficult – indeed it might be thought well-nigh impossible – to get right. How am I who have no mathematical competence, cannot read a graph, and cannot understand the technical terms of economics for any longer than it takes to explain them to me, how am I to choose between the programmes of the political parties?

The answer is, presumably, that one must find out who the relevant experts are and pay attention to what they are saying. It is to the credit of theologians (in their lay capacity) that they are readier to do this than most of their academic colleagues. How often one hears theologians remark, on the Doctrine Commission or elsewhere, 'We must be prepared to listen to what the biologists, sociologists, economists, literary critics – even the philosophers – are saying.' And theological writing often bears witness to the assiduity with which this listening has been done. But I wonder if enough account has been taken of the hazards involved in listening to what the experts are saying. Here are some of them.

1. When one listens it is sometimes apparent – surprisingly often in my experience – that what they are saying is nonsense. Why this is so I hope to discuss shortly; that it is so can scarcely be gainsaid. Not long ago I heard a distinguished literary critic developing the thesis that nothing which an author says in a work of literature can be expressed in words other than those actually used by the author. In other words interpretation and translation are impossible. I objected that some works of literature, such as Plato's or Hume's dialogues, are also philosophical exercises and that a basic philosophical procedure, to make sure that an argument has been understood, is to rephrase it carefully and then ask its proponent, 'Does this represent what you want to say?' No philosophy undergraduate would be allowed for one moment to get away with the rejoinder, 'No, what I want to say can be said only in

the words I actually used in my essay.' What the lecturer had done, it seems to me, was to generalise illegitimately a thesis which is true in the special case of lyric poetry (and perhaps, to some extent, in other sorts of poetry). Another instance is provided by the method adopted by some biblical critics, according to which, if one wants to discover what a historical individual thought, one must discard anything attributed to him which is characteristic of the tradition in which he stood and also anything that is characteristic of the tradition he initiated: what is left is undeniably his. One has only to apply this method to any of one's contemporaries to realise that the resulting account of his beliefs would be grotesquely distorted. Once again what has been done is to take a procedure which is appropriate to a very specific situation – when there is reason to believe that none of one's sources can be trusted and when one requires a high degree of certainty in one's conclusions – and extrapolate from this to historical study in general. Austin Farrer scarcely exaggerates in his verdict upon much New Testament criticism: 'Great systems of organized folly take the field and establish themselves as the academic orthodoxy of the day. To the detached observer the theological and the philosophical bias animating much of this work is obvious.'[1] (It is only fair to add that he once referred, in my hearing, to his own 'exegetical extravagances'.) I am tempted to add as a further instance of the nonsense talked by experts anything at all said by structuralists or deconstructionists, but I fear that I should then myself be generalising from insufficient evidence. No doubt in all such cases there is something to be said in defence of the expert, but it can scarcely be denied, I think, that the layman can often catch the expert out in palpable errors. One is reminded of Mrs Kirk's comment upon her husband's activities as a moral theologian: 'Kenneth[2] spends a great deal of his time thinking of various subtle and sophisticated reasons for doing things that we all of us know to be wrong.'

2. That experts are capable of talking nonsense is not an accident. It is associated with certain pervasive features of academic life. Academic subjects, with few exceptions, are

inherently controversial. Hence experts disagree, and they tend to disagree systematically. Schools of thought develop and their supporters organise themselves in a quasi-political fashion in order to promote some distinctive way of defining and developing the subject. It may become important to capture particular posts, and sometimes entire departments may be subjugated or desperately divided. Hence academic discussion readily becomes polarised; and those who would sensibly occupy the middle ground generally lack the temperament required to lead and inspire a party and strike fear into the ranks of the enemy. So when the layman listens to the experts, it will make a decisive difference which experts he listens to, and it will not be the most sensible who make the most noise or whose utterances are most effectively amplified in the public arena.

3. Not only do the experts within a subject differ, more or less systematically, at any one time, but patterns of dominance change over time. Academic subjects undergo regular revolutions, with the consequence that whatever the experts are saying now they are likely to be unsaying in twenty years' time. Anyone who, like myself, is on the point of retirement, will have lived through one or more such revolutions. When I first examined in Greats in the early 1950s it was still customary for the ancient historians to pay the philosophers half a crown for every time the three philosophy examiners gave an agreed mark on the logic paper. This was a vestige of the years, just then coming to an end, of the so-called 'revolution in philosophy', during which experience had shown that pre-positivist philosophers and post-positivist philosophers had radically different views as to what constituted an acceptable answer in logic. Payments ceased during my term as an examiner. The revolution had been successful and no dissidents remained. My impression is that a similar situation is beginning to develop again as the traditional humanistic approach of Oxford philosophy comes under increasing pressure from more severely analytical, quasi-scientific American influences. At the outset of my teaching career Logical Positivism was still in the ascendant and it was almost

impossible to get a hearing for the rational discussion of religious claims. At the same time the dominant tendency in theology was a neo-Barthian insistence that the revealed Word of God was to be received in dutiful obedience and that natural theology was impossible. Had I listened to the philosophers at that time I could not have remained a Christian. Had I listened to the theologians I could not have become a philosopher – or not, at any rate, a philosopher of religion. Since then Sir Alfred Ayer, in his television conversation with Bryan Magee, has, with engaging candour, confessed that nearly all of what the Logical Positivists believed was false;[3] and it is very difficult to find a theologian prepared to defend the claims of revelation in any but a distinctly Pickwickian form.

4. A further problem for the layman derives from the way in which the academic subjects that show promise of helping him the most enjoy at best a somewhat precarious status within their own disciplines. The philosophy of religion, for example, is one among a number of branches of philosophy in which one might reasonably aspire to become expert. Any academic is used to being asked the question (usually by visiting Americans), 'What is your field?', and if he answers, as I do, 'The philosophy of religion,' the expectation is created that there is a recognisable set of important issues upon which he will, more or less confidently, pronounce – arguments for the existence of God, the nature of religious language, time and eternity, the problem of evil, and so on. However, as soon as he undertakes to supervise graduate students working on any of these topics, he becomes aware that the student will need to spend much of his time exploring some other branch of philosophy, confirmation theory for the nature of explanation, philosophy of language for types and uses of metaphor, and so on. And when the thesis comes to be examined, there is an appreciable danger that it will be judged altogether as an exercise in confirmation theory or philosophy of language. Care needs to be taken, for this reason, in the choice of examiners, for there are some philosophers around who believe that questions in the philosophy of religion

simply resolve into questions in some more fundamental and, as they would think, more respectable branch of philosophy; and others, a shade more liberal, who hold that the philosophy of religion, although conceptually a distinct enterprise, is one that ought not be ventured upon until the more basic philosophical groundwork has been completed.

This state of affairs is not, of course, confined to philosophy. I was recently asked by a Danish friend if I could recommend to him a good history of England, and I passed on the question, naturally enough, to a historical colleague. I became aware at once that I had, unwittingly, committed a dreadful solecism. 'A history of England!' he repeated incredulously, as if he could not believe his ears, 'A history of England!' 'But *I* wouldn't know about things like that. *I* only read archives and monographs.' So J. H. Plumb writes, after acknowledging the essential importance of this specialised work:

> Specialization has proliferated like a cancer, making detail vivid, but blurring the outlines of the story of mankind, and rendering it almost impossible for a professional historian to venture with confidence beyond his immediate province. And that can be very tiny – the Arkansas and Missouri Railway Strike of 1921; the place names of Rutland; twelfth century Rouen; the oral history of the Barotse; the philosophy of Hincmar of Rheims. And so it becomes ever more difficult for the professional historian to reach across to ordinary intelligent men and women or make his subject a part of human culture.[4]

Thus academic disciplines are subject to a process of indefinite atomisation, and the relentless atomiser, when presented with a thesis, however narrowly circumscribed, can always discover some more basic problem which the writer ought to have disposed of first.

5. The problem is further exacerbated when one starts to listen to experts in different subjects at the same time. The layman (especially, perhaps, if he is a theologian) is inclined to expect that there will be, at least, a scientific consensus. For

is there not a scientific world-view, and is it not of crucial importance that theology should accommodate itself to it? But those sciences which matter most to the theologian, *viz.* those which bear upon the nature of man, are the theatre of an unresolved struggle between biologists and sociologists (with the psychologists uneasily in the middle); the former maintaining that there is indeed such a thing as human nature and that it is, in all important respects, controlled by the genes; the latter asserting the supremacy of culture over nature. For the sociologists this is a struggle for their very existence as practitioners of a recognised discipline, for, if the biologist's claims are allowed, sociology is reduced without remainder to sociobiology.

Further along the road, so to speak, on another boundary, is a longstanding dispute between sociologists and historians, the former asserting, and the latter stoutly denying, that history is in the end applied sociology. Thus theologians who are persuaded that they ought to conform to the requirements of 'scientific history' are faced by continuing controversy as to what the expression means, and what its implications are for historical research.

I hope I have said enough to show that the layman's task is not a happy one, if he resolves, as it seems he must, to listen to the experts. It is bad enough to discover that wherever he treads he is trespassing upon the preserves of one or more experts, and there is nowhere he can call his own; much worse to find that, in place of a territory neatly laid out in however complicated a pattern, he is venturing upon a battlefield, upon which frontiers are fiercely contested as the struggle ebbs and flows across them.

Thus situated, what should the layman do?

1. In situations of difficulty there is often much to be said for doing nothing, and this is the first option I propose to explore. Doing nothing does not mean, in this context, trying to have no opinions, since this is manifestly impossible. We all find ourselves, at any given time, with a large body of opinions, upon which we rely and which, we trust, are reasonably coherent. The policy I have in mind is that of continuing

to believe whatever one happens to believe now. Let us call it 'methodological conservatism'. As a policy it has certain evident advantages:

(a) We each of us know what we think; we are familiar with it and we are at home with it.

(b) It has got each of us where we are without manifest disaster. To that extent experience favours it; and it is, moreover, our own experience. We have, to a greater or lesser degree, been 'nourished' by the convictions we have already got.

(c) It has the merits of what Burke called 'prejudice', of which he wrote: 'Prejudice is of ready application in the emergency; it previously engages the mind in a steady course of wisdom and virtue, and does not leave the man hesitating in the moment of decision, sceptical, puzzled, and unresolved.'[5]

All three of these are good reasons for not giving up one's present beliefs, whatever they are, whenever the balance of evidence or argument appears to tilt against them. A certain tenacity in believing must be accounted an essential intellectual virtue. But a general policy of inexpugnable prejudice is exposed to three fatal objections:

(a) One's prejudices may not accord with truth – indeed it is obvious that, since people's prejudices conflict, many will be more or less false. Alain Peyrefitte, in his acute and entertaining book *Le Mal Français*, accuses his countrymen of preferring preconceived theory to the evidence of their senses, and tells of a French airman in May 1940 who observed a column of German tanks heading eastward not far from the Belgian frontier in the neighbourhood of the Ardennes. This was duly reported to headquarters, who told him he must have been mistaken. He then took up with him his Commanding Officer, who was a trained observer, and (flying dangerously low to be sure of the markings) together they saw, now, two columns of German tanks. On returning to base the CO himself rang headquarters, to be told quite firmly: 'Our military strategy is based on the postulate that German tanks cannot penetrate the Ardennes forest. Therefore, whatever you saw down there, it cannot have been German tanks.'[6]

(b) The man who is prejudiced on principle is deprived of free and unfeigned intercourse with his fellows. I cannot enjoy human companionship with you if I am determined in advance not to pay attention to anything you say or take any of your arguments seriously. Hence one of the marks of incipient marriage breakdown is the complaint of either party, 'He/she never listens to anything I say.'

(c) One's beliefs will ossify unless one is prepared to modify them in the light of criticism. Indeed they are likely in the course of time to lose the character of belief altogether and become a sort of conditioned reflex. We all know people who, upon receipt of a suitable stimulus, will recite opinions which they have long ceased to think about and which we no longer pay any attention to. But if one is prepared to modify beliefs at all in the light of criticism, one cannot set arbitrary limits to the process – one may be compelled to revise them radically or even to abandon them.

2. At the furthest extreme from methodological conservatism is thoroughgoing or Swinburnian rationalism. Richard Swinburne in his recent book *Faith and Reason*, the third volume of his impressive trilogy on the philosophy of religion, lists five kinds of rational belief. I will not go into the detail of his exposition, but will content myself with explaining the nature of 'rational$_5$ belief', which is the most adequate sort. Thus S's belief that p is rational$_5$ belief 'if and only if S's evidence results from past investigation which was adequate and inductive standards which have been subjected to adequate criticism, and S has investigated adequately whether his evidence makes his belief probable'.[7] Swinburne notes that

how much investigation is adequate depends on the importance of the belief at stake; whether it is virtually certain that it is true or virtually certain that it is false; whether or not there is some probability that investigation will achieve results; and whether the subject has other important actions to perform.[8]

The thoroughgoing rationalist will – unless he has other important actions to perform – do everything he can to ensure that all his beliefs are well-grounded, and this will involve him in large-scale investigations together with rigorous examination of the inductive standards appropriate to each such investigation. It is clear that Swinburne regards rational$_5$ belief as a regulative ideal which it is neither possible nor reasonable for the individual to achieve. Given the state of affairs described earlier in this paper, it is evident, I think, that the rationalist who did attempt it would make virtually no progress – even if he were fortunate enough to have no other important actions to perform. Not only would he have to become expert in all the disciplines that have a bearing on, say, the nature of man, but he would also have to resolve satisfactorily the leading disputes between these experts, including second-order disputes as to the methods by which such disputes are to be resolved. He would also have to adjudicate in the numerous border disputes between exponents of different disciplines in such a way as to do justice to the data assembled and the procedures recognised by them. The task is totally unmanageable.

3. This being so, another posture suggests itself, that of suspense of judgement. This follows naturally from W. K. Clifford's often-repeated dictum: 'it is wrong always, everywhere and for everyone to believe anything upon insufficient evidence'.[9] Since, as we have seen, it is very difficult to attain sufficient evidence for most of our beliefs, and so satisfy ourselves that we have attained it, and quite impossible to do so for all of them, the proper attitude must be to suspend judgement. We cannot, of course, in practice suspend judgement about everything, and the sensible exponent of the principle will concede that we shall need a host of practically relevant beliefs, which we must come by as best we can. But his guiding policy is to reduce these to a minimum.

Suspense of judgement, however, although it seems at first sight to be an eminently reasonable policy, is open to two serious objections, both of which were classically formulated by William James in his famous essay 'The Will to Believe'.

There are some choices which cannot be avoided, between options which, in James' words, are 'living, forced and momentous'.[10] In matters of morality, politics, religion, we must either make conscious choices or live as if we had made them, and our whole life hangs upon the choice (this is the truth to be found in Pascal's wager). Moreover, even in the domains of pure science or scholarship, where suspense of judgement is often more appropriate, if discoveries are to be made, risks must be taken. A policy like Clifford's, which is designed to avoid error, is not well suited to discovering truth. There is need for an experimental faith.

4. If choices *have* to be made, and adequate reasons cannot be found, we seem to be left with only one possibility – existential decision. This, it seems to me, has all the defects and none of the virtues of methodological conservatism. The existential decision is not open to criticism – for nothing can *count* as criticism – and it lacks the support of long experience. Better far to hold on to nurse.

This, then, is the layman's predicament. He cannot ignore the experts, but neither can he wholly trust them; and the more obvious strategies open to him are none of them entirely satisfactory. It was my primary intention to describe and analyse this predicament, but I am aware that I shall be thought to have cheated if I make no attempt to get out of it. How is the intelligent layman to proceed?

1. He is entitled to take comfort from the fact that there is, at any rate, a mass of common-sense beliefs to which the experts are committed as much as he is. To this extent my earlier metaphor of enclosure is misleading. Every parish has some common land. The theories of the experts have to be tested and, in the last resort, they are tested against things that the layman knows. And these are things that for the most part the individual – be he layman or expert – has never investigated, and, were any single one of them to be investigated, it would be against a massive background of as yet untested assumptions. It is true that this common-sense area is subject to change (it used to be a matter of common sense that men cannot walk on the moon), but it changes very

slowly, and at any given time there will be much that cannot be called into question without undermining the very reasons advanced for doubting it. For this insight the layman is indebted to a surprising convergence in the arguments of Newman and Wittgenstein. Newman writes:

> We are all absolutely certain, beyond the possibility of doubt, that Great Britain is an island. We give to that proposition our deliberate and unconditional adhesion. There is no security on which we should be better content to stake our interests, our property, our welfare, than on to the fact that we are living on an island . . . it is a simple and primary truth with us, if any truth is such; to believe it is as legitimate an exercise of assent, as there are legitimate exercises of doubt or opinion.[11]

And Wittgenstein writes:

> I believe that I have forebears, and that every human being has them. I believe that there are various cities and, quite generally, in the main facts of geography and history. I believe that the earth is a body on whose surface we move and that it no more suddenly disappears or the like than any other solid body . . . If I wanted to doubt the existence of the earth long before my birth, I should have to doubt all sorts of things that stand fast for me.[12]

Hence the layman has a certain capacity to recognise nonsense when he sees it (although he just could be mistaken).

2. The layman is able to depend on what Burke calls 'the bank and capital of all ages'. That is to say he can, and generally does, rely on one or more religious or political traditions, and these organise the available information in a more or less coherent and defensible way; traditions whose 'bank and capital' he can draw upon, because it has been accumulated by others over a long period of time. Hence he can enjoy the advantages which Burke claimed for 'prejudice' – but, if this is not to be mere 'methodological conservatism' it must be, as Burke recommended, 'prejudice with the reason involved'. That is, the traditions he relies on must admit of criticism.

3. But how, it may be asked, is he to choose between rival traditions? The Swinburnian rationalist (*i.e.*, the individual who aspires to rational$_5$ belief) would insist upon an exhaustive survey of all the alternatives on offer, followed by careful assessment and decision. It is the manifest impossibility of this which constitutes the original predicament. But, in practice, a good deal less than this is needed. We all possess and can further develop a capacity for tacit, intuitive judgement, which enables us to tell whether a total position will or will not do, without there and then – or perhaps ever – being able to make our reasoning explicit. The expert often suffers from an inability to see wood for trees; the layman can often trace the outline of the wood without being able to pick out or describe the individual trees. And this can equip him to tell when the expert has yielded to the besetting sin of academics, that of preferring interesting falsehoods to unsurprising truths.

4. In this he is helped by the tendency for rival systems of thought to exemplify in a systematic way certain characteristic styles of argument. If the layman is himself expert in some one discipline and has observed these rival styles at work in it, he can often recognise them also in other disciplines. Two examples would be reductionism and relativism. The atomisation I mentioned earlier comes from assuming that academic disciplines form a hierarchy of such a kind that each one higher up can be regarded as, ultimately, a special case of the one immediately below it. And relativism is commonly a reaction to the discovery with respect to a particular discipline, that its procedures are not rational when judged by criteria appropriate to some other discipline.

5. This same capacity for implicit judgement operates in another way that is even more important for the rational choice of a tradition, that is, through the assessment of people. Here Newman is once again to the point:

> We judge for ourselves by our own lights and on our own principles; and our criterion of truth is not so much the manipulation of propositions as the intellectual and moral character of the persons maintaining them, and the

ultimate silent effect of his arguments or conclusions upon our minds.[13]

Both in politics and in religion we are rightly impressed by individual persons who in their character, conduct and habits of thought exemplify the characteristic features of the tradition.

The layman, therefore, is not entirely without recourse, and his best policy is to draw judiciously on each of the strategies I earlier dismissed. He will follow the methodological conservative in attaching considerable antecedent weight to the tradition or traditions that have nourished him. He will follow the Swinburnian rationalist in using his own critical capacities to evaluate the evidence so far as he can and judging traditions by their response to criticism. He will take from the existentialist a readiness to accept risks in order the better to discover truth, and he will learn from the old-fashioned, or Cliffordian, rationalist that it is sometimes best to suspend judgement; not all questions need to be decided now.

No academic can, in the end, recommend the layman to ignore the experts altogether. As an academic himself he must believe that in spite of the obsessional tendencies of academics, the difficulty they experience in getting the focus right, their subservience to fashion, their oscillations from one extreme to another, nevertheless they do, by a curious zig-zag path, approximate gradually to the truth. But, at any given time, as he listens to the experts, the layman will be well advised to take what he hears them saying with a grain of salt.

In my own practice, for what it is worth, I think I am, to use the traditional terms of moral theology, a probabilist rather than a probabiliorist. The probabiliorists held that one ought to follow the more probable opinion – that of the majority of reputable thinkers; the probabilists that one was entitled to judge for oneself so long as *some* reputable authorities were on one's side. If you were to represent me as saying that I prefer to trust those experts who reinforce my prejudices, you would not be altogether wrong.

2

CONTEMPORARY CHALLENGES TO CHRISTIAN APOLOGETICS*

C. S. Lewis was the greatest Christian apologist of his time, and his works still have a wide readership. In paying tribute to his memory nearly a quarter of a century after his death it would be entirely appropriate to discuss some aspects of his own writings. I propose instead to look at contemporary challenges to Christian apologetics from the standpoint of someone who is primarily a philosopher and who belongs to a generation later than Lewis'. There is a genuine element of continuity here, for I had the privilege of succeeding him as President of the University Socratic Club at Oxford, which he founded, and which for many years was one of the liveliest undergraduate societies in the University. And like all thinking Christians of that period, I owe him an enormous debt of gratitude. Although he was very well grounded in philosophy and taught the subject in his earlier years at Magdalen, he felt increasingly after the war that he was not equipped to take on the professionals and turned away from technically philosophical topics to theological questions of wider scope.

So I want to consider, first, external challenges, and then internal challenges to Christian belief as they have developed since Lewis' time.

---

* Originally read as the C. S. Lewis Memorial Lecture, Belfast, 1986. From the *Journal of the Irish Christian Study Centre*, forthcoming.

External Challenges

What I have in mind is this. In discussing external challenges to Christian belief we are concerned with providing a convincing statement of Christian truth to our contemporaries. To be convincing it must be presented in a way that takes account of the problems and pressures that affect people in their actual situation. I say problems *and pressures*, because people's difficulties are not purely intellectual – even the difficulties of intellectuals are not; and even the problems that are intellectual generally receive their particular pattern and emphasis from people's social and personal life. But the convincingness of a case depends enormously on the context in which it is presented; it will fail to convince, for example, if the presenters behave as if they didn't themselves believe it, or if they disagree radically among themselves in such a way that the disagreements do not appear to be fruitful, or if they escape disagreement by avoiding problems which their potential audience can see manifestly arising. To put the issue in a crudely commercial way, if one is trying to sell something to someone, it is wise not only to study the market and the competition, but also the product and its packaging.

At each stage in my discussion I shall try to distinguish the state of affairs in the academic world from that in the cultural world at large (in so far as one can make that distinction). So far as academic philosophy is concerned I think it is fair to say that the question of Christian theism has now returned to the status which it occupied before the Logical Positivist movement got under way. That is to say, the problem of God is seen once again as one of the great controversial issues of philosophy – together with the problem of free will, the problem of personal identity, the mind-body problem, and so on. I should guess that more professional philosophers are atheists or agnostics than are theists, but it is distinctly less of a surprise today to discover that an able philosopher is a theist than it was twenty or thirty years ago. Then it was still generally believed that it was possible to draw a reasonably clear line between science and common sense on the one hand

and metaphysics (including theology) on the other. Sir Alfred Ayer himself had gone so far as to reject belief in God as literally meaningless. This whole movement has now petered out, and philosophical critics of Christianity, although still prepared to argue initially that the concept of God is logically incoherent, are not as a rule determined to hold that line, but instead fall back on the claim that, as an account of the nature and character of the world, theism is not very probable.

The reason for this change is chiefly that scientific explanation itself has proved impossible to describe and account for along positivist lines. Both the reliance of scientists upon models and their need to posit unobservable entities in order to explain phenomena reveal analogies with religious thinking; and the considerations that lead a scientist to prefer one explanation to another (*e.g.*, simplicity, elegance, comprehensiveness, coherence, explanatory power) are recognisably of the same sort as are appealed to in trying to decide between world-views. Positivism could not give a convincing account of science; and a convincing account, when offered, failed to justify the positivist attempt to reject metaphysics, and with it theology, as a rational enterprise.

This means that when philosophers now attack Christianity they rely on arguments which are recognisably of the same general kind as the plain man uses. In particular they stress the difficulties for theism of accounting for the character and extent of the evil that there is in the world. This is far from being the sterile attack that the positivistic one was, leaving the Christian apologist merely bewildered; for he too can see the difficulty and has always lived with it; and a philosophical critique on these lines can actually help theologians to deepen and develop their understanding of Christianity. Some years ago I took the chair at a series of discussions about *The Myth of God Incarnate*[1] (subsequently published as *Incarnation and Myth*[2]), and I remember how the debate really began to become creative at the point where the participants seriously considered the question how far a doctrine of incarnation was required to give substance to God's involvement in human suffering.

The demise of Logical Positivism means also that rival world-views (*i.e.*, possible alternatives to theism) are liberated from the positivist ban on meaninglessness. Materialism as a metaphysical system was as philosophically suspect to the positivists as theism, and people who were, in effect, materialists used to have to disguise themselves as positivists in their attack on religion. Now there is no need for them to do so. So once again philosophers are in line with a general cultural movement. From the point of view of Christian apologetics this is a gain. For it means that the materialist alternative to theism (along with others) has to be spelled out and defended in detail and its implications made explicit. It is much healthier in every way for rival world-views to be recognised, and vigorously contested, for what they are, than for the sceptical critic to be free, as the positivists supposed themselves to be, to demolish the claims of religion without his own substantial views ever being called in question.

The main secular alternative world-views are, it seems to me, materialism (or scientific naturalism) and Marxism. In a sense, of course, they are not alternatives but variations of a single materialist theme. But both in theory and in their practical implications, and also in the attitudes that go with them, they are significantly different. Marxism has a quasi-religious character, which is apparent in its discernment of an immanent and inevitable purpose in history, and its demand for complete commitment on the part of its adherents; whereas scientific naturalism favours a pragmatic, sceptical turn of mind and a utilitarian approach to ethics. To the Marxist the scientific naturalist is a typical bourgeois product, characteristic of the capitalist West; while to the latter the Marxist is heir to most of the vices of religion, especially dogmatism and intolerance.

Through its insight into the way in which economic and social conditions interact with moral and political ideas, Marxism has contributed something essential to our understanding of society, but this insight provides no warrant for a total economic determinism. As a world-view (as distinct from a contribution to sociology) it has been largely discredited in the West (and indeed, increasingly, in the East too) by its totalitarian denial of human rights. This is not just an incidental feature of Marxist thought, but follows from its insistence upon viewing individuals not primarily *as* individuals but as members of a class. The working class has rights (which in capitalist countries are restricted or denied) but the bourgeoisie have not, since their claim to individual rights is but an expression of a false economic and political system, which is destined to be superseded. The belief in human rights is something which remains very strong in our culture and the Marxist denial of them is an effective bar to the wider acceptance of Marxism.

Scientific naturalism or scientific humanism, meanwhile, has its own problems. They centre on the nature of man and his freedom. The scientific naturalist has to hold that man, like everything else in the natural world, is a product of processes that are scientifically explicable; and it seems to follow that human choices could, in principle, be predicted, if only we knew enough about natural laws and the state of the world at any given time. The mind is to be identified with the brain, and mental events, including decisions, with physical changes in the brain. It is very difficult, both as a matter of logic and in imagination, to see how genuine freedom of choice can be ascribed to men so understood; and, if it cannot be, not only is moral responsibility threatened, but also rationality in general. This whole issue is one of intense philosophical controversy and of enormous difficulty. How *is* the relation between mind and brain to be understood in the light of modern knowledge? And what *are* the implications for theory and practice of alternative answers to the problem?

Clearly Christian thinking must come to grips with these problems and be prepared to attend carefully to the scientific evidence. And theologians with scientific expertise like A. R. Peacocke are in fact doing so.[3] This is, of course, the issue that C. S. Lewis addressed in his essay on *Miracles*.[4] At the more popular level the discussion is still thought of as being about science *versus* religion, but the issues are a good deal more complex than that. Part of the problem is that the sciences do not speak with one voice – the unity of science is more pious hope than accomplished fact. Not only do psychology and sociology make assumptions about human motives and intentions which are not reducible to physics and chemistry, but they often raise problems about the objective character of scientific enquiry itself. So the natural scientists, for so long accustomed to providing the paradigm of rational thought, now find themselves, disconcertingly, treated in a deliberately objective way, as examples of a social group with common interests. And these, it is held, to some extent determine the direction and the character of their enquiries. At the same time historians of science[5] are beginning to cast doubt on the legendary story of the growth of modern science which was the guiding theme of Bronowski's *The Ascent of Man*,[6] and Don Cupitt's *The Sea of Faith*.[7] In retrospect the familiar representation of the great scientific thinkers as engaged in a constant and eventually victorious war with religious dogmatism and obscurantism is seen to be highly misleading.

It is very tempting for religious apologists to welcome these developments and to assume that anything which appears to weaken the authority of science must automatically restore the credit of religion. This seems to me a great mistake. There is mounting evidence, as I understand it, that Christian theology was influential in the growth of modern science. It inculcated the belief that the world obeys laws which, because they originate with God, cannot be discovered simply by inspecting it, or simply by the exercise of human reason without careful experiment. The enormous labours of the early scientists were undertaken in the faith that the world has an intelligible structure which is there to be discovered. Christianity and natural science share a conviction that there is a truth which it is possible, although always incompletely, for men to attain to. No doubt some spokesmen for science have maintained that there are no truths but scientific truths and no explanations but scientific explanations, and we have a right to protest against such dogmatism, but to deny the possibility of objective truth altogether is as destructive of religion as it is of science.

Nevertheless, scientists do now find themselves threatened in an unaccustomed way. The foundations of science have been called in question and scientific method challenged in the name of cultural relativism. From this relativist standpoint our modern scientific world-view is only one among a number of possible options between which there can, ultimately, be no rational choice. Even our scientific medicine, which has the most dramatic achievements to its credit, is not, from this point of view, to be judged superior to 'primitive' magic.

In combating this kind of relativism, the scientist cannot simply rely on the authority of the scientific method itself – for it is just this that is being challenged. He has to appeal to criteria of rationality of a very general kind – simplicity, coherence, comprehensiveness, *etc*. – and, as I urged earlier, the same criteria can also be appealed to in favour of the claims of a religious system of belief to explain the nature and character of human experience. I suggest, then, that in the intellectual world at large, Christian apologetics has a tremendous opportunity. Positivism has ceased to be the force it was, Marxism as a world-view has largely discredited itself, and scientific materialism is confronted with serious problems as to its own consistency and ultimate justification. The situation is no longer one in which there is a thoroughly coherent and agreed scientific world-view based upon an unchallenged scientific method, but rather one in which the claims of science require to meet the same sort of sceptical challenge as religion has long been used to.

It is, therefore, much more difficult now to draw a simple contrast between the solid, common-sense reality of the world disclosed by science and the speculative uncertainty of religious claims. At the same time, because of the intellectual and moral uncertainty of this situation, thoughtful people long to discern some meaning in life over and beyond what they as individuals choose to give it. So there is more willingness than there has been for a long time to take the intellectual claims of Christianity seriously. This does not mean that Christian apologists can expect to secure a clear dialectical victory over their rivals by producing straightforward solutions to the problems that perplex people. It is rather that, because people do not expect clear-cut answers to many of them, they are more content 'to see through a glass darkly'.

At the popular level my impression is that things are a good deal less favourable. The tide that in the intellectual world is running in is here still running out. There is still a great deal of popular 'scientism', which is taken to 'disprove' religion, and which, more insidiously, erodes people's capacity to appreciate and understand the language of religion. Either religious doctrines are regarded as cut-and-dried statements of quasi-scientific fact, and promptly rejected as incredible, or they are treated as expressions of purely personal feeling. Scientism and relativism thus conspire to convince people that there is no truth in religion. Religion is either not true at all (because not scientific) or 'It's true for me' or 'It's true for him', a purely personal matter which no institution, and therefore no church, has any right to pronounce upon.

Sociologists of religion trace this phenomenon to what they call 'privatisation'. Peter Berger remarks on the need people have for 'nomoi' or meaning-systems in terms of which to order their lives (his views are summarised in a report on young people's beliefs):

'Nomos' activity may be expected to cluster around marginal situations – death, loss, change of status, crises, etc. None of this alters in its fundamentals in the modern world except through the impact of differentiation, fragmentation and privatization. The role of official bodies, and especially of churches and states, in providing and effectively purveying ready-made 'nomoi' . . . is greatly reduced because they lose their monopoly in conditions of pluralist competition. Meaning systems, moreover, are not mere intellectual exercises, but must be lived collectively; constant interaction with other people who perceive and interpret reality in the same way as oneself is necessary if one's 'nomos' is to be automatically effective in imbuing one's everyday experience with meaning. But modern societies have largely dissolved these supportive systems . . . and among them the churches. This happens when the individual in his multiple and fragmented role exists partly inside and partly at a tangent to so many institutions and associations that no one of them addresses itself to 'meaning' throughout the whole range of his life experience, but only to snatches and fragments. So in the end the individual is in a certain sense alone with the task of making sense of the world and his own place in it out of scraps and oddments culled here and there in his differentiated life and contacts.[8]

I suggest that this represents the greatest 'external' challenge to Christian apologetics in Western countries. There has been an increasing disintegration both of the older Christian culture and of the newer rationalist culture. This, for the time being at any rate, leaves many ordinary people, particularly young people, quite happy to adopt a pragmatic, utilitarian attitude to society at large, and to meet the crises of personal life with odd and often inconsistent scraps of 'philosophy' picked up from anywhere and claiming no universal truth or even relevance. The more thoughtful, however, feel increasingly the lack of meaning and purpose in their lives and are to that extent readier to take Christianity seriously, but they often have difficulty in identifying themselves with a continuing historical institution. The very conditions which create the need for meaning also make it extremely difficult to meet it.

Internal Challenges

I have suggested that the decline of positivism and its attempt to draw a sharp line of demarcation between science and metaphysics (including theology) has enabled theism to emerge once again as a world-view with a claim to be taken seriously. Given that materialism and theism are again live options (as for a while they were thought not to be) it is not enough for the critic of religious claims simply to challenge them from the sidelines without in any way otherwise committing himself: he has to enter the arena and defend his own position, whatever it is. The Christian apologist, for his part, needs to decide where he stands in relation to 'modern knowledge' and to present a coherent statement of Christian doctrine which takes it into account. This does not mean, of course, that he has to solve all the problems – the present age is conspicuously one in which many problems have to be left unsolved – but it does mean that he has to know what the unsolved problems are and why it is reasonable to adhere to Christian belief in spite of them. Reflective people are, I think, readier to listen to such a statement than they have been for a long time.

My own impression is, however, that, often when given the opportunity to explain Christian doctrine and its implications to a potentially receptive audience, theologians have little definite or distinctive to say. This is not at all surprising, for the 'acids of modernity' have been at work here, too, and the intellectual problems facing theology are considerable, as are the social and psychological pressures upon the clergy. In a situation in which the foundations of science are thought to be problematic, the foundations of theology are unlikely to be undisturbed. Whatever the reasons, and however understandable they are, the fact appears to be that there is a broad divide between conservative and liberal (or radical) opinion, which is the source of considerable weakness. Neither party adequately meets the external challenges to Christian apologetics. The conservatives fail through not addressing themselves sufficiently to the task of relating the historic Christian faith to modern knowledge, including the results of a critical study of the Bible. Hence their apologetic, though vigorous and uncompromising, and worthy of respect on that account, is of limited appeal, and strikes many reflective enquirers as intellectually inadequate and even at times dishonest. The liberals, on the other hand, have been too much inclined simply to take over what they suppose to be the 'modern scientific world-view', which reduces Christianity to a sort of deism. Religion is thus seen, as it was in the television series

The Long Search, as the story of 'man's religious quest', and concepts such as those of 'revelation', 'grace' and even 'incarnation' are reinterpreted entirely in terms of human religious experience. This evokes from the interested non-believer the sort of response that was well expressed by a philosophical colleague of mine: 'The trouble with Christianity as presented in so much modern theology is that it isn't worth disbelieving!' The reflective non-Christian feels intuitively that Christianity, if true, radically transforms our ordinary view of the world and of human possibilities. This trend in liberal theology has been greatly influenced by the philosophical legacy of Hume and Kant or, more broadly, of the Enlightenment. They were believed throughout the nineteenth century (and well into the twentieth) to have undermined theism as an explanation of the existence and character of the world and of man's place and purpose in it, so that Christianity has to be understood as an expression of man's religious experience or of his existential decision to endow his life with meaning. Schleiermacher and Bultmann illustrate these approaches. One might say, in very general terms, that theology drew heavily upon the categories and attitudes of the Romantic movement, with its emphasis upon authenticity and its suspicion of claims to objective truth. Anglo-Saxon theology has been, characteristically, less extreme in this respect, but it too has been reluctant to countenance any notion of God's activity in the world other than through the naturally explicable processes of nature and of human cultural history. Here the decisive influence has been the discipline of biblical criticism, which has led theologians to suppose that only those influences can actually have been at work in the history of religion which an entirely secular thinker is prepared to discern. Hence it is very widely believed that a theological doctrine, such as that of the incarnation, can in no way be based on historical evidence. The historian, it is said, can *qua* historian, take account only of purely natural events and can offer only entirely natural explanations of them. Hence explanations in terms of divine activity must either be disallowed altogether or, if introduced at all, be based upon faith alone. The possibility that the whole episode might, when carefully and sympathetically studied, be such as to make a theological interpretation more convincing than any entirely naturalistic one on offer, is not even brought into the reckoning. Underlying this is an unspoken assumption that a scientific world-view is mandatory upon the theologian.

Now it may be the case that, when all things have been considered, the naturalistic explanation is to be preferred, but, for reasons that I gave earlier, it is no longer possible to rule out a more definitely theistic interpretation from the start. The strictures directed by Hume and Kant and other thinkers of the Enlightenment against theological explanations have turned out to be equally fatal to scientific explanation; and there does not, at present, exist a scientific world-view possessing the unchallengeable authority that many liberal theologians wish to give it.

I do not want to give the impression that the theological task is currently an easy one and that one certain philosophical inhibitions or prejudices prevent a contemporary *Summa* from being developed. But I do think it is a weakness of what I have broadly called liberal (as distinct from conservative) theology that it is not prepared to explore more boldly the conceptual possibilities for a distinctively Christian metaphysic that modern philosophy affords. So I would myself like to see Christian theologians stop for a while reflecting on how *difficult* it all is and actually address themselves, in specifically Christian terms, to the questions their unbelieving contemporaries so insistently ask, as in his day C. S. Lewis did.

A corollary of this is that conservative theologians should be more prepared to enter the general theological debate. Their reluctance to do so is to a large extent due to a suspicion that, once criticism is admitted on any terms, it will eventually take over, and the essentials of Christian faith will have been surrendered. And, in the light of some trends in 'liberal' theology, this suspicion is not wholly unreasonable. It is, in fact, the reverse of the coin. Both sides tend to assume that criticism can be exercised only in a secular way leading to sceptical conclusions. But, once this assumption is challenged, the way is open for a critical conservatism – an element which is not entirely unrepresented in the present theological scene, but is nevertheless somewhat under-represented.

Nor, I think, can the conservatives claim to be themselves entirely free from the influence of the scientism which has so markedly affected the liberals. It appears, as James Barr has argued, in the extremely literal manner in which the language of Christianity has often been interpreted, a literalism which is in contrast to the readiness of the Church in earlier ages to recognise the symbolic and poetic character of much religious language.[9] Here is another case in which theology can benefit from closer contact with the world of secular thought, in this instance that of literary criticism.

But it has to be recognised that freer and livelier debate between Christian theologians, radical and conservative, is not likely to result in a consensus. And the question has to be asked, how far this absence of consensus must reduce the effectiveness of Christian apologetics.

A great deal must depend on the character of the debate. It can be fruitful given two conditions. One is that it can be seen to concern things that matter; so long as this is so, lively controversy is a sign of health and its presence helps to persuade potential believers that they are not being asked to leave their intellectual consciences behind if they come into the Church. The other is that the Church (I am using this in its broadest sense of 'the whole company of faithful people dispersed throughout the whole world') has itself some rationale available of the differences within it. At present we have no such rationale. We are liable to regard it as a scandal that Christians do not entirely agree as to the content of their faith or as to its implications.

Obviously there are, and always have been, differences due to lack of charity or lack of thought, but it may be that there are two kinds of difference that are not attributable just to these causes.

1. If it is conceded, as I think it must be, that attempts to

formulate Christian truths and to put them into practice can never be entirely adequate – the transcendent cannot be wholly captured in finite terms – theologians are bound to draw upon the most suitable philosophical systems available; and the practical implications of Christianity are bound to be worked out in relation to the prevailing social and economic possibilities. (This can be avoided to some extent by the faithful withdrawing into small communities cut off from the intellectual and moral influence of the world, but this is not an *ideal* solution either.) This situation encourages the development of variant traditions, each of which emphasises some features of Christianity at the expense of others. It could well be that a fuller and richer approximation to the truth is achieved in this way than by an attempt to reconcile these different traditions by means of some compromise formula. This does not mean that genuine reconciliations are not sometimes possible (and should be sought as far as possible); only that a certain tension between variant traditions may be of positive value.

2. There is another distinction within the Christian Church which needs to be recognised and understood, *viz.*, that between the main body of Christians and the advance guard of theologians or 'the scouts'. If it is true that the Christian faith needs to be brought into relation with the best thought of the day, it must be someone's task to do this, and this task is bound to be to some extent exploratory and experimental. It is debatable how much freedom the 'scouts' ought to have, but, unless they have a good deal of freedom, they cannot do their job. It is worth remembering that even St Thomas Aquinas' massive development of Christian theology in terms of Aristotelian philosophy (later to become an established orthodoxy) was at the time regarded with considerable suspicion. No doubt there are risks attached to theological exploration, but, unless the risks are accepted, the result will be ossification, and that is worse. The fact, then, that there are these differences within the Church ought not to be regarded as a weakness, but as a sign of vigour. To develop the military analogy, the scouts and the main army ought not

to be attacking one another, but rather concentrating upon the defeat of the enemy.

When one acknowledges these two sorts of division, between different traditions and, within each tradition, between the main body of the faithful and the theological explorers, another image suggests itself, that of a river. The main stream sometimes divides into several large streams and a number of smaller ones, some of which later feed back into the main stream, while others continue to run parallel to it indefinitely. Some of these streams represent secular currents of thought which have Christian origins and which later contribute once again to the main flow of Christian thought. The 'secular thought' of a culture deeply influenced by Christianity is unlikely to be entirely secular, and it is possible that certain ideas that are genuinely Christian may be, for a time at least, preserved and developed better in a secular medium than in the mainstream of Christian theology.

I conclude, then, that lack of full agreement in the interpretation of doctrine need not weaken the apologetic stance of the Church, and can indeed strengthen it, so long as church members themselves learn to appreciate the value of diversity. Having said this, however, it is important also to insist that *diversity should not be accepted for the wrong reasons.* Earlier in this lecture I mentioned the relativism that is so striking a feature of contemporary culture. People are very much inclined to say 'It's true for me' or 'It's true for him' and to resist the idea that truth is independent of the beliefs and attitudes of individuals. Sociologists associate this with the conditions of modern life, in which social arrangements are made in a purely pragmatic, utilitarian way and the search for meaning and truth becomes a purely private affair.

The prevalence of this attitude is, as I said then, one of the greatest threats to any Christian apologetic, and we ought to be wary of it. My impression is, however, that many of the more articulate Christians, those who belong to synods and equivalent bodies, are themselves strongly tempted by it. It appears in the ready welcome they give to the concept of 'the plural society'.

The philosophy underlying the plural society is generally this. There is a distinction to be made between, on the one hand, a basic social morality, which can be justified pragmatically – society could not survive if it were not observed – and, on the other hand, a morality of individual ideals, which is purely personal in inspiration. The basic social morality is founded upon certain broad non-controversial facts about human beings and what is capable of harming them; personal ideals derive from 'visions of life' which have no objective basis but which owe their existence to the creative imagination of individuals. Religion, on this showing, belongs to the realm of personal ideals, and has no claim to objective truth. It follows that there should be complete freedom for people to preach and to practise their religion, so long as they do no tangible harm to others or to society at large, and so long as they do not seek to influence the basic social morality. Different religions, of course, reflect different 'visions of life', and all are to be tolerated, and indeed up to a point welcomed, so long as they are prepared to accept the purely private status they are offered.

This philosophy of the plural society fits very well into the sociological framework I was mentioning earlier, and it is entirely understandable that Christian apologists, especially those in exposed positions, should be inclined to take it over. Faced by a social situation in which it is increasingly difficult to persuade people to accept any religious or moral authority, it is reassuring to learn that it would be morally and religiously improper to claim any such authority. It is nice to be able to say: 'In our increasingly plural society the Christian cannot claim any special authority or influence.'

But, if the sociologists are right, it is the felt unsatisfactoriness of just this sort of 'plural society', with its increasing 'privatisation' and its restricting of meaning to the purely individual realm, that affords the Christian apologist his chief opportunity. Simply to embrace the philosophy underlying it and to offer the Christian gospel as one among a range of possible options, none of which has any serious claim to truth, is to add to the patients' malady, not to cure it.

This means, of course, that we need to rethink the Christian basis for a liberal society, in which the rights of individuals and communities are founded upon a Christian understanding of man which is widely shared by non-Christians. It is not adequate to regard Christianity as a purely personal matter having no social implications. The case for freedom is based not upon the absence of any reason for preferring one ideal to another but upon the positive conviction that men have the right and the duty to follow their consciences and to promote the common good. It is no more likely in politics than it is in the institutional life of the Church that we shall achieve a Christian consensus. Christians will continue to differ in their political emphasis, and it may be a good thing that this should be so. But in each case there is an overriding demand for the exercise of charity, not only out of consideration for others but also out of concern for the truth which transcends our best endeavours to define it.

3

IS THERE A DISTINCTIVE CHRISTIAN ETHIC?*

The question before us is a very complex one, although it looks at first comparatively simple.

It could be treated purely empirically: do we in fact find that Christians differ from non-Christians in moral theory and practice? But, as in all such empirical investigations, we run up at once against awkward problems of definition. By what criteria are we to determine who are to count as Christians; and how do we discriminate between aspects of thought and conduct that are 'moral' and others that are not properly so-called? Any answers that we give to these questions will be more or less controversial, themselves reflecting theological, philosophical and ethical assumptions.

Hence we may as well admit from the start that, in attempting to answer the question, we shall need to take a line on disputed matters of theology, moral philosophy and normative ethics. The line need not be arbitrary – we shall hope to make out a reasoned case for it – but we shall have to recognise that the case is unlikely to remain unchallenged.

If people are asked whether religion makes any difference to morality, they will generally regard the answer as obvious. The truth is, however, that it will be found, on further questioning, that some take the answer to be obviously 'Yes' and others take it to be, equally obviously, 'No'. Those who take it to be 'Yes' are not, on the whole, intellectuals. Intellectuals, whether believers or unbelievers, are inclined,

---

* Originally read at an Anglo-Scandinavian Conference at Lincoln, 1979.

for varying reasons, to give the answer 'No'. Theologians are reluctant to adopt a position which might seem to be unacceptably 'triumphalist', as suggesting that Christian doctrine yields moral insights not equally available to the purely secular moralist. And philosophers have been impressed by a particular argument, or family of arguments, purporting to show that there can, as a matter of logic, be no distinctively religious ethic. Neither position is greatly helped by the degree of confusion about morality, its scope, character and content, that is discernible as much among philosophers and Christian theologians as among the public at large. There is very much less of a moral consensus even in a comparatively homogeneous country like Britain than there was. If there is a pattern of morality upon which all reasonable men may be presumed to agree it is by no means easy to recognise it; and if there is a distinctively Christian ethic, that also is increasingly hard to identify.

In endeavouring to chart 'the theological frontier of ethics' one may start either from the theological or from the ethical side. That is to say, one may try to discover the ethical conclusions which follow from a chosen theological position; or one may look for a defensible theory of ethics and consider how, if at all, theology could have a bearing upon morality, given the truth of this theory. A 'theological position' will include some account of the scope, character and content of theology, and a theory of ethics will similarly embrace an account of the scope, character and content of morality. There are dangers in starting from either end, but they are, perhaps, greater in starting from theology. For theologians may proceed from theological premises which, when their implications for morality have become clear, are seen to deny morality the sort of autonomy it ought to have, or to fail to make sense of morality as a human institution, or to generate conclusions about how one ought to act or what sort of person one ought to be which run counter to our deepest ethical intuitions. Of course, if one starts from the ethical end, there are some comparable dangers too. One may develop a theory of ethics which, by its very structure, prevents one from giving due weight to theological considerations in matters of morality. Nevertheless morality as a pervasive human institution has a broadly recognisable shape, which is regularly studied as a subject of interest in itself by philosophers, social scientists and others without reference to religion, and it makes for simplicity to assume, at least at the outset, that it can be treated as independent of religion. No doubt in the end one will need to some extent to call in question one's initial assumptions, but it is reasonable to do so only when they have been given a run for their money.

Moral philosophers in the analytical tradition have tended to operate with two contrasted conceptions of morality. According to one of these an individual's morality consists in the answers he gives to the question 'How shall I live?' and these will suffice to constitute a morality, so long as certain formal conditions are satisfied. Chief among these are that he should be consistent (*e.g.*, be prepared to recommend to others that they should act in given circumstances as he believes that he should act) and sincere (*i.e.*, actually behave in the way he claims to believe he ought to behave). The individual adopts a particular morality through the choices (explicit or implicit) that he makes. Large numbers of individuals may make broadly similar choices and, in so far as they do, one may speak of the morality not just of an individual but of a group or a society. When a morality has permeated a society for long periods, it is likely to affect its language, so that certain moral conceptions become 'incapsulated' in the language men habitually use. Nevertheless the emphasis in this philosophical approach is individualistic; for, however strongly entrenched in a society certain moral conceptions may be, they have authority over the individual, and so represent for him a morality at all, only in so far as he freely and responsibly assents to them and actually lives by them. It is evident, I think, that this way of conceiving morality has affinities with Romanticism: what matters more than anything else is that the individual's choices be genuinely authentic. Of course, human nature being what it is, there will be considerable overlap between the ways of life chosen by different individuals (quite apart from the influence of the 'incapsulated' standards already mentioned), but there is no strictly logical reason why someone should not repudiate traditional morality altogether and do so from a genuinely moral standpoint.

According to the other approach, morality is essentially a social institution, designed to enable men to avoid the dangers and frustrations that would flow from the expression of unrestrained self-interest. Hence for an individual's answer to the question 'How shall I live?' to count as a moral one, it is not enough that it be sincere and consistent; it is necessary also that it be supported by reasons, and these reasons must relate to the needs or wants of men in society. Otherwise an individual's policy for living is no more than simply his own policy for living and, as such, may well be immoral rather than moral. This way of looking at morality includes, but is not confined to, most utilitarian theories. One might say that its tendency is rationalist rather than Romantic.

It is sometimes argued that the difference between these two conceptions of morality is of verbal interest only, a matter simply of how one chooses to use the word 'moral', but I think that there is more to it than that. Confronted by the phenomenon of morality, one is bound to ask what the purpose or point of morality is, and on the face of it the second conception provides an intelligible and defensible answer to this question, whereas the first does not. When one considers the most typical injunctions of morality – those whose recognition is well nigh universal – one cannot fail to be struck by the fact that they are precisely such as are needed to prevent human life becoming, in the familiar words of Thomas Hobbes, 'solitary, poor, nasty, brutish, and short'. One cannot conceive a human society existing, or remaining in existence, without a morality of this kind, so that, as Plato remarked, even a band of robbers requires justice of a sort, if it is to have the minimum coherence necessary for achieving its purposes.

I propose at this point to be somewhat dogmatic and make it clear that this latter conception of morality seems to me clearly preferable to the other. In terms of it one can account for the requirements of sincerity and consistency which the other approach emphasises, for moral principles will not perform their social function adequately unless individuals treat each other impartially and assent to them sincerely. And it allows morality a social function which it plainly has.

But this account of morality is so far extremely sketchy, and it remains to be seen how it can be filled in. If it were to turn out that only one set of moral principles, virtues, types of argument, *etc.*, could fulfil the social purpose which morality has according to this view, we should have arrived at a complete and non-controversial system of ethics which would be entirely independent of religion and leave no room for a distinctive Christian ethic. If this is not the case, it remains possible that Christianity makes a difference to ethics of a kind that may be very fundamental. All we have so far learned is that, in asking what difference, if any, Christianity makes to ethics, we are asking what difference it makes to the scope, character and content of an institution whose function it is to enable human beings to realise their purposes and fulfil their needs by accepting certain restraints upon how they might otherwise behave.

C. S. Lewis, in a stimulating essay entitled *The Abolition of Man*,[1] claimed to discern in societies of widely differing kinds what he called 'the ultimate platitudes of Practical Reason', and I shall in what follows use the expression 'the Platitudes' to refer to those moral conceptions which are to be found in all, or virtually all, moral codes. The Platitudes often receive little attention because, as Platitudes, they are not particularly interesting, especially to intellectuals who relish individuality and distinctiveness. But that one should tell the truth, keep promises, show gratitude for benefits received and make reparation for injury, refrain from killing or injury without just cause, act fairly and observe at least a measure of reciprocity in one's dealings with others, punish only the guilty and make the punishment commensurate with the offence; these are moral requirements that are so widely accepted that, where any one of them is denied, one looks for some special explanation of the fact. Anthropologists, for example, have noted that honesty is not always rated as a virtue in societies where magical practices are endemic – because, presumably, in such circumstances it may be thought better for the truth to remain concealed from those who might make harmful use of it. Also among the Platitudes are, arguably, certain prohibitions which relate to the institutions of property, marriage and the family. It is wrong to cheat and steal, to commit adultery, to fail to honour one's parents or care for one's children. The *rationale* of all this is well stated by A. M. Macbeath in his survey of the anthropological evidence in *Experiments in Living*:

> [Any] form of social life requires that there should be rules governing the relations between persons in regard to such matters as intercommunication, return for services rendered, sex relations, respect for life and property, etc., and that they should be generally obeyed. And the rules contained in lists of *prima facie* obligations are in general such obvious conditions of individual and social well-being that most of them are included in the moral codes of most peoples.[2]

That there are moral Platitudes and that this is their *rationale* seems to me undeniable. If on closer investigation there was found to be general agreement as to their scope, character and content, they would constitute a complete system of morality of such a kind as would render otiose any distinctively Christian ethic or, indeed, any ethic deriving from some specific world-view. The Platitudes would, in that case at least, exhaust the possibilities of an objective, rationally defensible system of ethics, 'morality' strictly so-called, although there would be room for conceptions of a broadly ethical kind, alternative ways of answering the question 'How shall I live?', which individuals or groups would be free to adopt or not as they chose; and Christians might characteristically adhere to a particular set or sets of such 'personal ideals'.

Much depends, then, upon how exhaustive and how

determinate the Platitudes are. There are, I suggest, three main possibilities.

1. That they yield an objective and rationally defensible system of ethics which can, in principle at least, be understood and accepted by everyone, and which is complete enough to exclude the possibility of a distinctive Christian ethic. This possibility has been worked out philosophically in a number of different ways. Intuitionists have maintained that the Platitudes are discerned by a process analogous to sense-perception or to mathematical intuition. Kant believed that there existed a rational process – the principle of categorical imperatives – by which one could arrive at all, and only, the precepts which are binding upon all rational beings. The traditional Natural Law doctrine sought to achieve the same result by reflection upon the natural ends which a man, *qua* man, must be presumed to have. Scientifically minded utilitarians have relied upon some version of the principle of utility to generate a platitudinous morality. None of these, with the possible exception of Natural Law theory as developed by Aquinas, has thought it necessary or indeed possible to invoke religious insights in support of moral Platitudes.

2. That they yield a basic social morality which is, so far as it goes, rational and objective, but which is, to a greater or lesser extent, incomplete: either because it does not extend to the whole of what is recognisably moral, although it provides determinate answers within a limited area; or because it is rarely or never completely determinate, but requires further specification in terms of conceptions that are not themselves platitudinous. This possibility has been interestingly discussed by Professor Sir Peter Strawson in a paper entitled 'Social Morality and Individual Ideal',[3] and is implicit, I think, in the work of many contemporary Anglo-Saxon thinkers, such as Herbert Hart and Sir Isaiah Berlin. From this liberal standpoint Christianity may well furnish 'individual ideals' which complement the Platitudes and are in competition with rival ideals which complement them differently. A liberal society will characteristically tolerate and, indeed,

welcome this variety of moral ideals, while taking care to deny them any rational basis and any authority over the life of a society at large. This is what is sometimes meant by the expression 'the plural society'.

3. That the incompleteness of the Platitudes is of such a kind that, in order to function as the developed morality of any society, they require to be further specified in accordance with the same criteria as have been used in arriving at them; that is, in accordance with a set of more definite notions as to what human needs are and how they can be met in a society. On this view Christianity, or any other world-view, inevitably affects our ideas about morality, because it affects our conceptions of what men need and of what men are. Some human needs are so obvious and so exigent that they are all but universally recognised – hence the Platitudes; others are not. And even the obvious ones can be understood and appreciated at very different levels of profundity.

It will by now, I think, have become apparent where my own preference lies, and in what remains of this paper I shall try to justify it. I want to suggest that the Platitudes, although of the utmost importance and on no account to be neglected, do not in themselves suffice to provide an adequate morality; also that the liberal proposal to supplement the Platitudes by acknowledging a realm of individual ideals which give meaning to the individual's life but lack the rational support or the social authority of the basic social morality, is seriously incoherent and palpably unable to do justice to the character of Christian ethics and the claims it makes.

The Platitudes are generally justified in two different ways. The commonest is by reference to the necessary conditions for the existence of a viable society. The Platitudes comprise those principles and dispositions of character which need to be developed if men are to succeed in living together without their society disintegrating. The advantage of this sort of validation is that it is simple and, within certain limits, incontestable. Its disadvantage is that the morality that can be based upon it falls very evidently short of what our moral intuitions demand. Comparatively low standards of honesty, for example, and very rudimentary conceptions of justice may suffice for the survival of a society. Most historical societies have been characterised by patterns of privilege which most of us would now regard as unjust; yet some of them, such as the Hindu caste system, have survived for centuries. The alternative is to base the Platitudes upon some determinate conception of human needs and to rule that the needs of everyone in the society must be given equal weight. This is intuitively far more satisfying, but lacks the straightforward non-controversial basis that the other criterion provides. There is room for controversy and for appeal to ideals of human excellence which need not be universally shared. The Platitudes, that is to say, require to be interpreted in more specific ways. Thus it is a Platitude of a very obvious kind that any moral code must recognise some concept of justice and that any such concept involves the notion of reciprocity, but it is not an equally obvious Platitude that all men have equal rights.

The Platitudes are limited in yet a further way. It is a Platitude that a society needs some regulation of sexual behaviour, that is to say some version of the institution of marriage; and also some regulation of the control of resources, some version of the institution of property. But many different forms of these institutions may adequately discharge the primary role of enabling individuals to live together in a society. The Platitudes as such do not determine which of these various alternatives should be chosen. Moreover the Platitudes, though universally recognised as important, are not in all situations regarded as of *overriding* importance, and opinions may differ as to what other, non-platitudinous, values can override them and in what circumstances. In aristocratic societies, for example, respect for life – a platitudinous value – was often subordinated to the demands of personal honour – a non-platitudinous one.

Given the insufficiency of the Platitudes, taken by themselves, the liberal proposal is to encourage individuals or groups of individuals to remedy it by developing and expressing personal ideals within the shared framework of a basic social morality, taking care to prevent any such ideal engrossing the entire moral system of any society. For personal ideals are from this point of view not capable of rational assessment, but express the varying aspirations of individuals. The trouble with this position, as it seems to me, is that the clear distinction which it proposes, between a basic social morality that applies to all and is rationally defensible and an array of personal ideals whose authority derives solely from the choices of those who embrace them, cannot be sustained. When every allowance has been made for purely 'vocational' ideals which represent what an individual may aspire to in virtue of his individual temperament or endowment, most moral ideals to which men seriously subscribe are based upon conceptions of human excellence which they are prepared to explain and defend. Hence there is not a clearly recognisable break between the morality of the Platitudes and the morality of personal ideals. Both are related to human needs. What makes the Platitudes platitudinous is simply that the needs upon which they are based are particularly plain and obvious, and even these needs may be variously interpreted in the light of different ideals of human excellence.

Ideals of human excellence, in their turn, are affected by the views that are held about the nature and the predicament of man, in other words by world-views. Hence we should expect that Christianity would yield important moral implications that are distinctive to the extent that it possesses a distinctively characteristic doctrine about the human condition. It is, of course, conceivable that some other world-view should yield exactly similar moral conclusions, but this is, nevertheless, highly improbable.

My answer then, at this stage, to the question 'Is there a distinctive Christian ethic?' is that one would expect there to be. If morality is bound up, in the way that I have suggested, with the needs of man in society, and if one's view of such needs is related to one's conception of what men are, any system of belief that is at all comprehensive will tend to develop its own characteristic ethic. To be an ethic at all it will need to exhibit a certain structure and to contain some features which Strawson calls 'humanly necessary' – the features I have referred to as the Platitudes – but beyond these limits it will have its own distinctive character.

At this point it would be reasonable for you to ask, 'What, then, is this distinctively Christian ethic, and in what way is it characteristic?' It is a question which I am bound to try to answer, in however rudimentary and tentative a fashion. There is an obvious difficulty in doing so, which has already been touched upon at an earlier stage and can now be rendered more explicit. Christianity is not, and never has been, entirely monolithic. At any given time there have been conflicting doctrines – or, at any rate, conflicting interpretations of doctrine; and over the centuries doctrine has undergone change – or, at any rate, development. If, then, there is the relationship that I have been claiming between doctrine and ethics, these doctrinal differences will have been reflected in ethical differences. So any attempt to identify the differences that Christianity makes to morality is bound to be, to some extent, controversial – to involve taking sides in contemporary theological and ethical debates.

1. The first difference that Christianity makes, as it seems to me, is that it offers an answer, not otherwise available, to the question 'Why be moral at all?' The question can, of course, be answered up to a point in terms of the social function of morality. If it is true that the individual cannot achieve his purposes, or indeed become a person at all except in a society of some kind, and that no society can survive without some system of morality, the individual has an interest in the maintenance of that system and may reasonably be expected to play his part in maintaining it. But it is open to him, nevertheless, to be a 'free rider' and to be parasitic upon a system which benefits him, while discharging his obligations to it only to the extent that it is prudent for him to do so. This is the possibility to which Plato gave classic expression at the beginning of the *Republic*. But if it is God's purpose for man that he can achieve ultimate blessedness only in the love of God and of his neighbours in the Communion of Saints, he cannot in the end hope to prosper in a policy of self-interest.

The hope of such blessedness is not self-interested in any objectionable sense, for he desires it for others as well as himself; and, if he does not, he has not yet made the required *metanoia* – he has not repented.

2. The second difference is that it gives the demands of morality a categorical character which they cannot have in a purely secular context, and which is independent of the *de facto* preferences of individuals or social groups. Morality is more than a social contrivance or the expression of an individual will; it is, in some sense 'required by the universe'. It is true that this judgement assumes the failure of Kant's attempt to derive the categorical imperative from the nature of rational will itself, but it is my conviction that Kant relies far more heavily than he supposes upon certain assumptions that can only be adequately defended in terms of some kind of theism.

3. The third is the emphasis upon love as the supreme virtue and the consequent insistence upon the value of the individual personality. This is a familiar theme and a controversial one. It would be absurd to maintain that this conviction is in our culture confined to those who accept the Christian conception of God. It is now so widely diffused that it tends to be regarded as more indubitable than any metaphysical construction. Yet Christianity does provide a framework within which this conviction is intelligible and defensible, and it is surely not an accident that the most intense and persistent awareness of the value of the individual person, and the respect due to him, no matter how weak or ugly or insignificant in human terms he may be, has been found in conjunction with the worship of a Creator who has made man in his image and loves all men equally, and of a Redeemer who gave his life that all men might be saved. Our conception of human personality shows clear marks of its Christian origin. It may be the case that it can survive independently of Christian belief and that there is some alternative world-view which will in future provide the same sort of theoretical backing for it as Christianity has so far given. Such a possibility cannot be ruled out, but we are

entitled, I think, to ask for something more than the bare conceivability of such an alternative. Meanwhile it is clear that the ways of thinking about men and women that are most characteristic of contemporary naturalism or 'scientific humanism' are very hard to reconcile with the claim that they are irreducibly valuable.

4. There are those who would maintain that love is not just the primary but the only ethical conception of any importance that is distinctively Christian and that the remainder of Christian ethics is straightforwardly derivable from it. Indeed most of the ethical disputes among Christians today would appear to turn on this issue. The debate illustrates the way in which moral and metaphysical questions are mutually interdependent. There is no doubt that, as a matter of history, Christian morality has been influenced by, on the one hand, a tradition of Natural Law and, on the other hand, ideas derived from the Bible, and neither of these influences can plausibly be regarded simply as specifications of a single agapeistic imperative. The situation has been complicated by the association until very recently of Roman Catholic moral theology with a particularly inflexible interpretation of Natural Law, and of much Protestant moral thinking with a somewhat uncritical use of the Bible. Theologians, anxious to repudiate their old errors, have tended to react against both these elements in the Christian tradition by embracing a variety of personalism which consorts well with the pervasive Romanticism of the prevailing secular culture and involves comparatively little metaphysical commitment.

At this point, the desire to avoid 'triumphalism' also makes itself felt, to reduce so far as possible the dependence of Christian moral thinking upon conceptions not equally available to the secular mind and to conduct ethical enquiry in a vocabulary that is so far as possible neutral. My impression is that, on the Continent of Europe, this vocabulary may well be Marxist, whereas in the Anglo-Saxon world it is likely to be predominantly liberal.

The dispute shows itself particularly in relation to two large areas of moral concern, questions of life and death, and sexual behaviour. With regard to euthanasia and suicide, for example, there is a broad division between those who insist that men and women hold their lives in trust from God and may not, therefore, dispose of them as they see fit; and those who argue that the only relevant imperative is that of compassion, and that whoever disposes of his own or another's life (with due respect for the individual's wishes and the legitimate interests of others) is doing the will of God so long as he is guided by compassion. Similarly in sexual matters there are those who regard human choice as constrained by an understanding of the nature and purpose of human sexuality as intended by God, and as discernible through Scripture or the Natural Law, or both; and those who see it as God's overriding will that men should be free from all such constraints and seek only to give expression in their sexual behaviour to genuine personal love.

Mention of this dispute, which I have only sketched in outline, reminds us that if the main argument of this paper is sound, the same factors that make for a distinctively Christian ethic will also make for distinctively different patterns of Christian ethics. Hence in trying to formulate a Christian view upon a contemporary moral issue it is often necessary to debate questions which are not, strictly speaking, ethical at all, but concern doctrine, hermeneutical principles and, in a broad sense of the word, philosophy. Those who wish to appeal to the Bible as a unique source of moral insight seem to be committed to a comparatively strong doctrine of revelation; and those who rely on Natural Law to a particular understanding of creation. Both involve the espousal of theism as a metaphysical system in something like its traditional form, in which it makes sense to talk of the divine purpose in creation and of God making his will known to men by some form of communication with them. Indeed both rely upon a notion of divine action and are required by it. No doubt all of these concepts are to be understood analogically, but if they are to be viable, the analogies, although stretched, cannot be entirely sundered.

So, to sum up. A consideration of morality as a human

institution, with no initial reference to religion, suggests that it is essentially concerned with the recognition and encouragement of those principles and dispositions of character which are necessary for men's satisfying their needs and realising their purposes in a society. Some of these needs and these purposes are so universal and so fundamental as to yield a 'platitudinous' morality that is discernible in all, or virtually all, moral codes. But the morality of any developed culture goes well beyond these 'Platitudes' in at least two ways. It specifies them further where they are open to divergent interpretations, and it introduces moral notions which are not platitudinous at all, notions which are often connected with particular institutions which are characteristic of that culture. These developments in morality are systematically related to conceptions of what men need, which vary in the same sort of way, and are in turn influenced by prevailing views about the nature and predicament of man. Hence one would antecedently expect that any world-view which carries with it important implications for our understanding of man and his place in the universe would yield its own distinctive insights into the scope, character and content of morality, and it is not surprising to find that Christianity does so. To answer the further question 'What *is* the distinctive Christian ethic?' is inevitably to be involved to some extent in controversial questions of Christian doctrine and general metaphysics.[4]

4

SHOULD THE LAW BE CHRISTIAN?*

I take it that this question concerns the extent to which Christian considerations should influence the content of the law. A straight 'Yes' answer to the question would imply that, in a Christian country, the law should, so far as possible, embody Christian values. A straight 'No' would imply that the law should be strictly neutral so far as religion is concerned and that Christian values, as such, should not be reflected in it.

The actual situation in England conforms to neither pattern. It is largely taken for granted that the views of the churches (especially, but not exclusively, those of the Church of England) will be taken seriously when law-making is concerned with recognisably moral issues, but the churches are given no prescriptive right to determine the content of the law. This is so even in those cases where the law does impose duties in respect of religion, *e.g.*, in the religious education clauses of the 1944 Education Act; or in cases where the interests of the churches are straightforwardly involved, as in relation to Sunday observance.

It is an untidy arrangement and, for that reason, not easy to describe or defend. If it is defensible, this is most likely to become apparent from an investigation of the alternatives, which are, for the most part, altogether clearer and simpler.

As so often happens, the more extreme positions gain much of their plausibility from the assumption that together they exhaust the possibilities, so that the manifest errors of each

* Originally read at a conference of the Society for Christian Ethics, Oxford, 1986. From *The Month*, March 1987, pp. 95–9.

are taken as conclusive arguments for the other. The doctrine that the law should be morally and religiously neutral is a repudiation of the claim that 'error has no rights' and the licence *it* affords to religious majorities to ride roughshod over the consciences of those who dissent; while that doctrine itself is maintained as a needed defence against the moral subjectivism that is thought to be associated with any sort of liberalism.

The view that the law should enshrine Christian values is implicit in the Book of Common Prayer, where rulers are exhorted to 'the punishment of wickedness and vice and the maintenance of thy true religion and virtue'. It is assumed that there is one true religion and an objective moral law, and that it is among the duties of the state to promote both. In the Catholic tradition before Vatican II it was commonly held that civil society should promote the common good and follow the natural law, in such a way as not to frustrate the individual's aim of eternal salvation. It follows that, if all or most of the citizens profess the Catholic religion, the state too must profess it. Since 'error has no rights', citizens of other religions have no right publicly to profess their religions, though the public good may require toleration.

On this view the right of the state to embody Christian values in legislation depends upon the claim that the Catholic Church proclaims the one true religion, but is subject to the qualification that all or most of the citizens must freely acknowledge that religion. It does not imply that any other religion should enjoy a similar status, should it be accepted by the majority – for it would not be the one true religion. Hence this position is to be distinguished from that of Lord Devlin, who has argued that Christianity provides the values which *de facto* prevail in our society. He instances the law of marriage:

In England we believe in the Christian idea of marriage and therefore adopt monogamy as a moral principle. Consequently the Christian institution of marriage has become the basis of family life and so part of the structure of our society. It is there not because it is Christian. It has got there because it is Christian, but it remains there because it is built into the house in which we live and could not be removed without bringing it down. The great majority of those who live in this country accept it because it is the Christian idea of marriage and for them the only true one. But a non-Christian is bound by it, not because it is part of Christianity, but because, rightly or wrongly, it has been adopted by the society in which he lives.[1]

It is clearly implied that, if England were an Islamic society, the values reflected in the law should be Islamic ones.

The diametrically opposed view, that the state should be religiously neutral, is commonly associated with the concept of a 'plural society'. This too is formulated in two ways: philosophically, and also more pragmatically. The philosophy underlying the plural society is an accommodation between moral subjectivism and moral objectivism. There is a public morality, which is 'public' in two senses: that it derives its validity from public criteria – the need to sustain a viable society; and that it is properly applicable to everyone (for everyone has an interest in the maintenance of public order). There is, in addition, a private morality, and this also is 'private' in two senses: it derives what authority it has from the private preferences of individuals and it exercises that authority only over those who freely subscribe to it. In a sense the private morality is primary, because men are conceived as essentially self-creators, and their good is what each individual chooses to make of himself. In so far as there is a conception of the common good, it is strictly limited to the necessary conditions for the achievement by individuals of their own personal ideals. It follows that religion could not and should not affect the common good. It belongs in the private sphere. No doubt any religion has a social dimension, but its proper sphere of influence is to be confined to voluntary co-operation by like-minded people.

But the plural society need not rely on this extreme form of philosophical liberalism. It may be based instead on the *de facto* diversity of a particular society. If individuals and groups differ as to what is good, it is not in practice possible or desirable for legislation which is to apply to all to be determined by some particular conception of the common good. The function of the state can only be to maintain a structure of public order which is neutral as between the varying conceptions, *a fortiori* between religious systems. This more pragmatic position could be adopted by someone who holds that there is, in fact, one true religion, and is doubtless accepted by many Roman Catholics in the United States. It is, in principle, consistent too with the argument of Lord Devlin; it simply maintains that some societies are not sufficiently homogeneous for his prescription to work in practice.

The philosophical versions of the opposed positions are not, however, compatible, and I have suggested that one of the motives for adhering to each of them is a fear that otherwise one is committed to the other. The Roman Catholic pre-Vatican II political theory as developed in the nineteenth century was put forward in conscious opposition to liberal theories of the state, which were taken to imply indifferentism about fundamental values. Because it followed from indifferentism that there was no one true religion and that the state should be neutral in religious matters, and because indifferentism was held to be false, it was easy to assume that, since there was one true religion, the state ought to be guided by it in framing legislation. Similarly, the philosophical version of pluralism is in part a reaction against the authoritarianism and paternalism associated with the other view. Supporters of both positions share a major premiss, *viz.* that if there is a truth about the common good, and that truth is known, the legislator is entitled to embody that truth in legislation without further question. Authoritarians accept the antecedent and also the consequent. Pluralists are led by abhorrence of the consequent to deny the antecedent.

We have, then, in terms of our original question 'Should the law be Christian?', four possible answers so far.

1. Law should be Christian, because it is the function of law to promote the common good and Christianity gives us true insight into the common good.

2. Law should be Christian (in this country at least), because the law needs to reflect a common morality, and our morality is Christian.

3. Law should not be Christian, because it is the function of the law to reflect a public, utilitarian morality only, and religion belongs to a sphere of purely private morality.

4. Law should not be Christian, because there is not, as it happens, sufficient agreement about a common good to warrant any attempt to secure it by legislation.

I have argued elsewhere[2] that the philosophical form of liberalism or pluralism (point 3 above) is, in spite of its wide currency, untenable for the following reasons.

1. The basic common 'public morality', defined as those values whose acceptance and sufficient practice is necessary to the survival or viability of any society, is not sufficient for the well-being of any particular society. In particular, any society needs institutions, like those of marriage and property, which are such that:

(a) various forms of them are possible;
(b) no one form is, as such, necessary to the survival of *any* society;
(c) every society needs some form of them.

Hence, for example, monogamy and private property are institutions which a society which has them cannot do without, but which are plainly not such that every society must have them. But, if this is so, each society will have to choose which form of the institutions of marriage or property it intends to have, and legislate accordingly.

2. It is not possible to maintain the crucial distinction between public and private morality, the one a matter of rational public debate, the other of purely private preferences. Decisions about sex and the family, for instance, have profound social effects and are subject to vigorous debate; yet they are regularly assigned to the private sphere. The protection of human life is pre-eminently a concern of the state and is listed as such in any catalogue of principles of public morality; yet controversies about abortion and euthanasia illustrate the extent to which convictions about it reflect

religious and other 'philosophical' influences. It seems, then, that a society has no alternative but to make certain moral decisions which presuppose some ideal of human excellence; and such ideals are frequently religious in character.

If this critique has force, it disposes of the *de facto* version of pluralism as well. A society cannot maintain itself in a tolerable state unless certain institutions are recognised and protected by law; and such institutions encourage and are supported by an associated morality, notwithstanding that some members of society may not accept it. Hence a more substantial framework of law is required than would be needed simply to ensure mutual tolerance of diversity.

Rejection of these two forms of pluralism does not, however, carry with it the admittance of religious considerations into the making of law. It would be possible to argue that, although moral considerations are bound to enter into the process (over and above those that are taken by pluralists to comprise 'public morality'), there are good reasons why an appeal to religious considerations should not be allowed. (On one interpretation of the United States Constitution this is implied by the requirement that there be 'no establishment of religion'.)

As has been suggested already, one such reason might be the risks inherent in the view, which is seen by some as the only coherent alternative to pluralism, that, in Christian countries, the Christian Church has a prescriptive right to determine the content of the law (point 1 above). We need to ask, then, whether this position is as dangerous as it is thought to be, and whether it is the only one available to those who are unwilling to answer an unqualified 'No' to the question 'Should the law be Christian?'

One danger which is often thought to attach to this position is that, if one religion, Christianity, is granted this status, it follows as a matter of logic that other religions must be allowed a similar status in countries where their adherents are in a majority. Hence Islamic law, for instance, is legitimated, some forms of which are marked by intolerance and brutality. Similarly, Christian regimes, both Catholic and Protestant, which in the past have exhibited the same objectionable features, must receive retrospective legitimation. This argument, however, fails to take seriously the claim that Christianity (as such or in its Roman Catholic form) is 'the one true religion'. The status accorded to the one true religion in countries where it has a majority cannot be universalised in the manner suggested, because other religions are, *ex hypothesi*, not the one true religion. (The past record of the Christian Church itself cannot, of course, be dismissed in this way.)

This argument may be countered by the claim that, while Catholic Christianity may in fact be the one true religion, there are no sufficient reasons for believing it to be so. And the more modest assertion that any religion which is believed to be the one true religion should have a comparable status can be universalised. But it is open to the proponent of the position to reject the proposition that there are no good grounds for preferring one religion to another. It cannot, at any rate, simply be taken for granted. Nevertheless, it may be insisted, there is as a matter of fact no general agreement as to which religion, if any, is the one true religion, so that in practice, if a privileged status is conceded to any one religion in any one society, it will be that much more difficult to resist such a claim when made by the adherents of some other religion in some other society. And this does, indeed, seem to be true.

It is, then, an argument of some force against any given 'theocracy' (if I may use the term as a convenient shorthand) that many theocracies have been barbarous and tyrannical, and some still are, so that to legitimate one (however mild in practice it may be) is bound to provide some support to the others. But clearly the main objection to the theocratic principle is a more direct one, which has, in point of fact, been made incisively by Vatican II's 'Declaration on Religious Freedom'.

The Declaration represents an attempt to found a liberal political theory upon Christian principles by rejecting the doctrine that 'error has no rights'. The fundamental principle appealed to is that of the dignity of the human person as known both through reason and through divine revelation: it yields the political principle that

> all men are to be immune from coercion on the part of individuals or of social groups and of any human power, in such a wise that in matters religious no one is to be forced to act in a manner contrary to his own beliefs. Nor is anyone to be restrained from acting in accordance with his own beliefs, whether privately or publicly, whether alone or in association with others, within due limits.[3]

This principle is later generalised so as to cover all conscientious action:

> In all his activity a man is bound to follow his conscience faithfully, in order that he may come to God, for whom he was created. It follows that he is not to be forced to act in a manner contrary to his conscience. Nor, on the other hand, is he to be restrained from acting in accordance with his conscience, especially in matters religious.[4]

A man's duty to follow his conscience implies a right to follow his conscience even when it is erroneous. Hence the older 'theocratic' doctrine that 'error has no rights' is entirely repudiated, and repudiated on specifically Christian grounds as well as on the basis of natural reason.

It is clear, then, that the four positions outlined earlier do not exhaust the possibilities. There is a further position, which is, philosophically, neither theocratic nor pluralistic and which is, so far, not committed to either of the *de facto* alternatives. It remains to consider what answer it offers to our initial question 'Should the law be Christian?'

The Declaration itself does not give a clear answer to this question, because it is open to different interpretations. The problem is that, as it stands, the general principle quoted above is quite impracticable. No legal system can operate effectively without requiring some people sometimes to act against their consciences or refrain from acting according to them. The most that can be claimed is that law-makers should avoid, so far as possible, legislating in such a way as to do violence to people's consciences. And this is, in effect, recognised in the Declaration when it adds the qualification 'within due limits'. This is developed later in the document in terms of the notion of public order, which includes an order of peace, an order of justice, and a moral order. Little is said in the text itself about the last of these, except that it involves 'the proper guardianship of public morality'.

But it is here, of course, that the difficulties accumulate. If it is conceded, as it seems to be, that the state has, unavoidably, a legitimate concern with public morality, should religious belief be allowed to influence in any way the determination of this public morality in so far as it is enshrined in the law? Charles Curran, in a published lecture on the Declaration, notes that 'the public morality is interpreted as the basic minimal standard required for life in society'.[5] And this seems like a statement of the 'philosophical' version of pluralism. But later in his lecture Curran indicates a different view:

> The criterion of public order applies in the area of what has often been called, although not with great exactitude, private morality . . . Even within the realm of public order, the gospel and the church have a significant interest, but the approach to these questions must always be in terms of the criterion of public order with its threefold content, and not in terms of morality as such. It would be disastrous to interpret these important distinctions as implying a total immunity from the influence of the gospel, religion and the church.[6]

If the Declaration is interpreted in this way, as I agree with Curran in thinking it should be, the answer it gives to our original question is that, in a democratic society, care should always be taken, so far as possible, to avoid making laws which those subject to them find conscientiously objectionable and to allow individuals and groups, so far as possible, to decide how they shall live. But since moral decisions have to be made in some areas as to the content of the law (*i.e.*, since the law cannot be morally neutral), it is both the right and the duty of Christians to enter into the public debate about these matters and seek to influence the outcome. They should not, however, have a prescriptive right, denied to others, to determine the outcome before any debate has taken place.

The discussion in this paper has so far been somewhat abstract. In the space that remains I should, perhaps, try to relate it to the situation in two countries which are alike in being broadly Christian, but have different constitutions – Britain and the United States.

The position in Britain (or, more precisely, England) is that which I outlined roughly at the beginning of this paper: 'It is largely taken for granted that the views of the churches (especially, but not exclusively, those of the Church of England) will be taken seriously when law-making is concerned with recognisably moral issues, but the churches are given no prescriptive right to determine the content of the law.' I described this as 'an untidy arrangement and, for that reason, not easy to describe or defend'. It means in practice that when changes to the law are under discussion on such matters as abortion, euthanasia, marriage and divorce, homosexuality, prostitution, *etc.*, it is customary to appoint a Royal Commission or other committee of inquiry to make recommendations, and the Christian churches are normally represented in their membership and are also invited or encouraged to send in reasoned submissions. The churches themselves may well already have set up their own working parties, and these (especially, perhaps, those set up by the Church of England's Board for Social Responsibility) will address themselves to the question what, in all the circumstances of the case, the law should be. They will, that is to say, take account of the fact, in framing their recommendations, that many, indeed most, of those who will be subject to the law are not active practising Christians. They will, therefore, not as a rule urge the government to 'make the law Christian' in a thoroughgoing way, but will instead recommend some degree of compromise which does, nevertheless, to some extent reflect a Christian judgement. Thus even those who would reject divorce entirely, so far as marriage in church is concerned, can see the need to accommodate it in the law of the land. And even those whose doctrine of Christian marriage is the most liberal would for the most part share the Church's concern that marriage, as recognised by the state, should be in intention lifelong. The Church of England still acknowledges a responsibility to the nation as a whole (and so, in Scotland, does the Church of Scotland), and for the most part people are content that it should do. It is probably true to say that anxiety about this untidy state of affairs is more frequently voiced within the churches than outside them.

In the United States the situation is markedly different, partly because it is a very much less homogeneous society, but chiefly because the United States Constitution forbids the establishment of religion. There are, therefore, (or, at least, there *prima facie* seem to be), constitutional reasons why the law should not be Christian. My impression is, however, that the issue is at present highly controversial. On the one side are those who adopt a pluralist position in one or other of its forms and claim that the Constitution is on their side; on the other are those who reject pluralism in either of its forms and argue that 'no establishment of religion' should be interpreted to mean not that religious voices should not be heard in the debates that influence the law-making process, but that they should not have any prescriptive right to determine the outcome. The First Amendment, which forbids an establishment of religion, also guarantees freedom of speech and of assembly, and it is arguable that these are worthless to religious bodies unless they carry with them the right to express a view on the content of legislation.

It would be unwise for someone who is not an American citizen to attempt to adjudicate in this debate, but it is permissible to consider the bearing of our previous discussion on the issue. If the arguments advanced against the philosophical version of pluralism are cogent, it would seem that the case for complete neutrality in the USA would have to rest on the *de facto* version. The case would have to be that there is so much religious diversity in the United States that laws affecting all Americans should have no religious content at all, that is to say that their content should owe nothing to religious considerations. Only in comparatively few instances would this criterion be straightforwardly applicable. One such instance would be prayer in public schools; only religious people want to pray and only Christians want prayer to be Christian. In most other cases where there are Christian arguments for legislation – about, for example, abortion, euthanasia, divorce, and the like – there are also non-Christian arguments for the same legislation, and sometimes they are substantially the same arguments. The principle of the sanctity of life, which Christians appeal to against the practices of abortion and euthanasia, is not peculiarly Christian, although it is arguable that it is more congruent with a Christian view of life than with any other. It would be absurd to proscribe any legislation that was capable of a Christian defence on that ground alone, if it was also defensible on other than Christian grounds. But it would also seem somewhat arbitrary to allow the non-Christian arguments to be given full weight while excluding the Christian arguments altogether from the debate.

There is, however, another consideration which underlies much of the discussion about these issues and which requires to be made explicit. Reluctance to allow a Christian voice, or Christian voices, to be heard is often due to a conviction that these voices will be dogmatic and intolerant. I have talked throughout this paper about the debate that precedes legislation, and I have argued that Christianity should not be excluded from the debate. But 'debate' suggests a process of rational argument, in which reasons are compared and evidence assessed. It can take place only between people who are prepared to be reasonable. But, it will be insisted, religion is not a matter of reason; it is a matter of faith and derives from a divine revelation whose authority is personal conviction or an ecclesiastical *magisterium*. Those who are guided by it may speak, but they will not listen. They must be excluded from the debate, because in effect they exclude themselves.

It is not enough to respond to this by way of a purely *ad*

hominem argument: dogmatism and irrationality are not confined to the religious; why should only their religious manifestations be proscribed? The objection is an important one, and religious institutions have often been vulnerable to it. 'No establishment of religion' was a justifiable protection against the excesses of the religious when allowed free access to temporal power. Part of the significance of the 'Declaration on Religious Freedom' is that it presupposes a readiness on the part of the Roman Catholic Church to argue its case in a democratic state and to acknowledge the rights of minorities. It can be read as offering from a Christian point of view a defence of liberal democracy as a system of government.

But, the objection may be pushed, *can* a religious body argue its case in a secular forum (*i.e.*, one that is not already antecedently committed to the religion in question)? *Either*, it may be said, it will rely on Christian premises, which, *ex hypothesi*, opponents will not accept; *or* it will employ purely secular premises, in which case the ensuing law will not be Christian. In neither case will any genuine debate have taken place between Christians and non-Christians. The dichotomy, however, is altogether too neat to be convincing. It presupposes that there is and always must be a complete discontinuity between Christian and secular reasoning. Certainly this can occur – if, for example, the Christian is an extreme fundamentalist and the secular thinker regards individual preferences as the sole basis for morality. But in the sort of Western society we have in mind the moral intuitions of those who are not religiously committed have been influenced by centuries of Christianity and the mainline Christian churches have for some time been at pains to take account of developments in the human sciences and in the humanities which bear upon the interpretation of Christian doctrine. In a period during which the narrowness of the official churches has often driven genuinely Christian developments into other channels, it is not in fact all that easy to determine which ideas are of purely secular origin. But, these cultural reflections apart, Christians would presumably want to argue (at least, many of them would) that the Christian revelation does not require us to interpret the nature of man in ways for which there is otherwise no warrant, but rather affords a deeper understanding of man as he essentially is. If that is so, there is room for a genuine exchange of ideas.

The position at which we have arrived is liberal rather than pluralist. It does not attempt the impossible task of drawing a strict line beyond which legislation should not go, thus excluding religious considerations altogether, but it does recognise a number of important constraints upon the law-making process. Among them are the following:

1. So far as possible, privacy should be respected;
2. It is bad to pass laws which do not command the respect of those who are subject to them;
3. Laws should be avoided which are likely to fail of their object or produce a great deal of suffering or other evils;
4. One should not, as a rule, pass laws which are difficult to enforce and whose application tends, therefore, to be patchy and inequitable.

These principles represent, in effect, a specification of the assertion in the 'Declaration on Religious Freedom' that 'the usages of society are to be the usages of freedom in their full range. These require that the freedom of man be respected as far as possible, and curtailed only when and in so far as necessary.'[7]

My answer, then, to the original question is that the law should be Christian to the extent that a Christian element in the law has been accepted after full enquiry and debate and so long as due account has been taken of the constraints placed upon the law by the requirements of individual freedom – with the rider that these qualifications and restraints are themselves warranted by a Christian doctrine of man.[8]

5

THOUGHTS ON THE CHURCH
AND POLITICS*

I recently came across, in a village church in Norfolk, a memorial brass with the following inscription:

> In Loving Memory of _____ Indian Civil Service, who was killed by a tiger while defending his natives
> 'Greater love hath no man than this that he lay down his life for his friends.'

It is reasonable to assume that this man died doing his duty, and that he thought of it as his Christian duty and shared the faith which inspired his family to quote that particular text.

The memorial has a period flavour (one which was communicated to us powerfully by the television series *The Jewel in the Crown*, based upon Paul Scott's *The Raj Quartet*[1]). We should not now refer to Indians as 'natives' and we should be unhappy about the paternalism of 'his' natives. And yet this man gave his life for 'his' natives, and can we be confident that we should do as much?

Confronted by this episode we become aware of two divergent responses, which reflect two opposing views about the relation between Christian faith and politics. According to the one view the influence of Christian faith is to be looked for in the believer's personal life. It is possible to live a good Christian life no matter what the social and political system one lives under. We are all sinners and our attempts to live out

---

* Originally read at a conference of the Society for the Study of Theology, Oxford, 1984.

the gospel will be incomplete and, indeed, more or less corrupt, but these deficiencies will be aspects of our own personal shortcomings. The little that we know of the individual here commemorated shows that he was a good Christian man, at least in the manner of his death.

But there is another view which requires us to have reservations. On this view the individual's moral character cannot be judged in isolation from the concepts and attitudes characteristic of the society in which he lives. To the extent that the society is corrupt, *he* is corrupt – unless in word and deed he dissociate himself from it. Since there is nothing to suggest that this man did dissociate himself from the values of the British Raj which he helped to administer, the most charitable judgement that can be made upon him is that he represented these values at their best, but that these values were flawed.

On one view, then, this man was a good Christian, though doubtless in some respects a sinner; on the other he must be judged a somewhat imperfect Christian because he was implicated in social and political attitudes that were less than fully Christian. How far he is to be blamed for this involvement is not here the issue, but rather how far he succeeded in living a Christian life. The former view is associated with the claim that the Church should 'keep out of politics' and seek only to inspire individuals to a deeply felt personal religion; the latter with a call to the Church to bring a Christian critique to bear upon public as well as private life. The former view receives expression from time to time in the writings of Edward Norman. He would urge, I think, in the present case, that it is in principle inappropriate to compare the liberal values of today with the more authoritarian outlook of the imperial past. To do so involves a sort of parochialism in time – an unwarranted assumption that the values we happen to hold in this country, now in 1984, are superior to or more authentically Christian than those of any previous age. At any given time the values generally accepted will be a function of the social and economic order then obtaining, and it is neither more nor less possible to live a Christian life under one such set of values than under another. What matters is the individual Christian's position *coram deo*. In much the same way Dennis Nineham has argued that Christian doctrine itself is inevitably formulated in terms of the thought-forms of a particular age and that those of different ages are largely incommensurable.[2] It is the relationship with God which matters (however that is conceptualised), and it is that relationship which the Church exists to maintain.

But Norman does not invariably maintain this relativistic view. He asserts from time to time that Christianity does indeed have social and political implications, although he is somewhat reticent as to what they are. The main burden of his argument in the Reith Lectures[3] was that today's church leaders, like many of their predecessors in the modern era, have allowed themselves to be seduced away from authentic Christian teaching by the secular world-views (and their associated moralities) favoured by the members of the 'intellectual establishment' with whom they so often associate. In the process Christian teaching has been 'diluted' or 'corrupted'. By this he could mean, simply, that what ought to be a purely personal religion has been wrongly interpreted as having political implications; but the preponderant impression conveyed, to my mind at least, is rather that Christianity has been wrongly identified with certain political positions; or has been taken, uncritically, to have political implications which are not the right ones. He would not, I am sure, for one moment deny, for example, that the long campaign to suppress slavery was genuinely Christian or that it sought to remove a manifest evil.

A more moderate form of this response is to insist upon the constraints imposed by historical circumstances upon the individual's attempt to live a Christian life. We do not, from this standpoint, have to say that there is nothing to choose between the moral values of, say, a Christian social worker of the 1980s, and a Christian magistrate of Tudor times in their treatment of the poor. There was no public office which the latter could have occupied which would have given him the opportunity for the kind of principled exercise of concern which is open to the modern social worker. He could exercise private charity; and, beyond that, he could show as much justice and mercy in the administration of a severe law as his office allowed. The law, and the social system which it served to protect, could not, practically speaking, be changed, and certainly not by any action on his part. He had to make the best of an imperfect system which has now been replaced by a very much better one.

The situation of the District Commissioner in the Indian Civil Service was, arguably, little different. His defence against a modern critic could take two forms. Most strongly, it might be argued that, given all the historical conditions, the system he helped to administer was in fact the best attainable. India had endured a succession of foreign invasions, of which the British was to be the last. If the British had withdrawn, nothing remotely like a unified democratic state was likely to come into existence. In the circumstances of the time an authoritarian, paternalist government of the sort the British instituted was needed, and, where so few were called upon to rule so many, the rulers had to be a cohesive class, remote from the indigenous inhabitants. Hence the attitudes which offend us today. We may agree that the State of India is better today than it was then, and that relationships between individual English people and Indians are far better now, freed, as they are, from the old taint of superiority and subservience. But it is just anachronistic to suppose that all this was either possible or (except as a long-term aim) desirable a century ago.

'Of course', the apologist will go on, 'the Raj was not perfect.' By this two things can be meant, and it is important to distinguish them. The first is that the British Raj, like all institutions, was a compromise. It achieved (and was, to some extent at least, consciously designed to achieve) certain goods at a certain cost, where the cost might be the sacrifice of other goods or the acceptance of certain evils. No system can achieve all desirable ends and do so at no cost whatever. It may well have been the case, for example, that in order to maintain security and protect individuals from exploitation and injustice, it was not possible entirely to dispense with powers of arbitrary arrest and detention. In maintaining what had to be, in effect, a gigantic bluff, a show of magnificence and a strict hierarchy of command may have been unavoidable, and so on. Yet imperfect as it was, in this sense, it is conceivable that the balance actually achieved was the best that *could* have been achieved in the circumstances. The judgement of history might be that the Raj, all things considered, did more good than harm to India, not least in providing the matrix for the development of a unified, independent, democratic state. This would appear to be, for example, the view of the Indian historian Nihal Chaudhuri. (Whether, even if true, this could justify the original process of annexation is another and more difficult question. But it can be offered as a justification for maintaining the system once it had come into being.)

But there is another sense in which it was not perfect. Even if the defence I have just sketched succeeds, and there was implicit in the Raj an 'operative ideal' worthy of respect, that ideal was not fully realised. Although there were individuals in all parts of the system who treated their subordinates as human beings and who did not equate social position with human worth, and among these were some who respected the riches of Indian culture and helped to explore and revive Indian art and literature, there were many others who did not, and who thought of themselves as representatives of an inherently superior race. Such attitudes are so insidious that they readily become institutionalised and thus, to some extent, affect everyone, whether they know it or not, whether they wish it or not. The tone of voice in which many would speak of 'natives' would infect the language itself, and it is this that we react to when the word appears on the memorial tablet.

This more moderate response largely concedes the critic's case and protests only against a naive and uncharitable form of it. It does not deny that Christianity has implications for social and political life or that a responsible Christian should be alert to them. It simply warns us to be aware of the inevitable complexities and ambiguities of politics. What the individual can do and, hence, what he ought to do, cannot be read off from a set of simple and universal principles, but depends upon the political situation he actually encounters and his individual role in it.

There is, in any case, an element of false antithesis in the contrast between personal life and political involvement. Personal life is not to be identified with private life. The District Commissioner who goes out to shoot a tiger which is threatening 'his natives' is not operating in some private realm. He is carrying out the duties of his station. But, if he is a Christian, he will be giving expression to his concern for fellow children of God. In all his relationships he will seek to be honest, just, merciful and courageous, and he will be moved not simply by abstract virtue but by love of his fellow man, and these relationships form part of a web of social and political institutions. The difference made to the operation of these institutions by the spirit in which the individual lives is very striking, not least in those where the structures are comparatively fixed and unchangeable, as in the armed forces. The individual who does not seek to change his role, or has no power to change it, can nevertheless discharge it in such a way as to treat all those with whom he deals with the respect due to persons – or not. Identical ships, or virtually identical colleges, can vary enormously in the quality of their personal relationships according as the occupants of key positions do or do not love their neighbours. 'Personal virtue' exerts an influence that goes far beyond the private sphere: so does personal vice. Hence Herbert Butterfield reflects: 'It is conceivable that it would have required no great change in human nature generally, but only a little less wilfulness in great masses of people at one time and another, to hold in check some of the more monstrous evils of the twentieth century.'[4] The 'personalist' can argue, moreover, that this must be the heart of the matter. To love one's neighbour, however much it may demand political action, must at least involve an active personal concern with whoever is one's neighbour here and now. This is a present anticipation of the Communion of Saints and it cannot wait until some time in the indefinite future, when needed social improvements have at last been made.

This emphasis is enormously important, but it is not enough, even within its accepted limitations. The good Christian who is content to operate entirely within the existing framework of his station and its duties is indeed required to exercise personal virtues in his situation, but this must mean appropriate personal virtues. A kindly well-meaning individual who has no feeling for the rights and obligations, the interests and susceptibilities of all the people working together in the institution, is not able to help its members effectively. The Christian who is a soldier or, for that matter, the Christian who is a don, needs to be a good platoon commander or a good tutor, and neither of these is a matter of routine performance. He will need to be guided by the 'spirit' of the institution, by what I called earlier the 'operative ideal', and it requires intelligence and imagination to become aware of it, whether explicitly or implicitly. Thus a tutor will want to help his pupils, but how it is appropriate for him to help them will depend in part on how their courses are structured. It may make a difference whether a system of continuous assessment operates or whether everything depends on a final examination. In one system tutor and pupil are entirely free to conspire together against the examiner; in the other the tutor *is*, to a certain extent, the examiner, and must scrupulously distinguish his roles. A simple willingness to help is not enough, whatever its motivation. To work effectively in the institution the individual needs to appreciate and appropriate its 'operative ideal'; and this being so, it is not surprising that different institutions produce different sorts of personalities in which different virtues are emphasised; and recognisably similar virtues receive expression in different ways when exemplified in different roles. I remember being forcibly struck by this when taking part in a conference on punishment attended by magistrates, police, lawyers and probation officers. The probation officers were concerned primarily with the rehabilitation of offenders, the police with the protection of the public, the lawyers with the rights of the individual, and the magistrates with all of these things but inclining in one direction or the other according to temperament.

Any morality, whether Christian or not, has to be a morality of 'my station and its duties', and so extends beyond a purely private sphere; and a morality which is *merely* a matter of 'my station and its duties' requires the individual to become aware of the 'operative ideal' of the institution (or institutions) within which he is working. As we have seen, any such ideal will represent an attempt to achieve the best possible balance of potentially conflicting aims and principles, and what the individual needs to understand is the rationale of that particular balance. But, in order to be able to do this, he must also be able to conceive of the balance being different. The thoughtful, reflective traditionalist is potentially the radical critic. And, as he reflects upon the values implicit in the system in which he is operating, he may come to feel that the balance is not right, that certain values are not allowed for at all or that others are over- or under-stressed. The impulse to criticise is likely to come from two different, though related, sources: his entire view of life, including, if he is a Christian, his Christian faith; and the experience of trying to work the system as one who adheres to that view of life. Thus he may discover that the military discipline he is called upon to administer is unjust or inhumane; or that the constraints imposed upon his teaching by the examination system prevent him from helping his pupils to develop fully.

I have taken examples from particular institutions rather than from the organisation of whole societies, let alone the relations between whole societies, because they impinge most unmistakably upon the individual as he seeks to give expression to his 'personal Christianity'. But it is obvious, I think, that no line can be drawn between these institutions and the wider society which may tend to uphold or threaten or challenge their values. We have to conclude, then, that, even if we start from the demands of 'personal Christianity', we cannot avoid the need for Christian concern with politics. The District Commissioner who, as a Christian, had a genuine desire to help 'his natives' cannot avoid, in principle, the question whether he could help them best by encouraging them to govern themselves.

The argument so far has reached a rather obvious conclusion, and one which does not, so far as it has gone, do much to help us decide how far the Church should pronounce on matters political. It rules out the extreme view that, so soon as a question has been identified as 'political', the Church should refrain from commenting on it, but it provides no criteria by which to decide what sort of comment is appropriate. (In what follows I propose to limit myself to the politics of this country and to the Church of England, which, because of establishment, is in a peculiar position. Some of what I say will, I hope, apply more widely, but it is best to acknowledge my limitations.)

When we speak of 'politics' we may use the word in wider or narrower senses. Sometimes we may think in terms of the familiar distinction between 'the state' and 'society', and regard as political only those matters in which the state as such is active – the apparatus of government, the administration of justice, the defence of the realm, *etc.* A very great deal that goes on in our social (*i.e.*, not entirely private) life is not political in this sense, including the activities of business and the professions, of voluntary associations, and so on. The limits of the state are more difficult to draw than they used to be because the state controls and regulates very much more of our social life than it used to; and it is among the major issues of political controversy just how extensive the state's involvement should be. What belongs to politics is itself a matter of political debate. Hence 'politics' has a different though related sense of those matters which are at issue between the political parties. The administration of justice, although a central part of the state's activity, and in that sense plainly political, is not for the most part an area of party political controversy and therefore not political in this further sense.

When people maintain that the Church should not 'meddle in politics', it is politics in this further sense that they chiefly have in mind. They do not hold that the Church should refrain from challenging, or from attempting to influence, the character of public life; indeed they would expect the Church to help set the standards of public conduct and condemn flagrant breaches of them; but the standards in question would be standards that all may reasonably be presumed to accept, and not those that are the subject of political controversy. That the Church should have, and should be seen to have, this role is an important element in the defence of the established Church.

The standards in question may be of a quite general kind, relevant to every sort of social activity, whether associated with the state or not: standards of honesty – freedom from corruption and deceit; of courage – refusal to yield to threats or popular or peer pressure; of humanity – concern for the needs of all the people affected by a policy or project; of fairness – a refusal to override the legitimate interests of any individual or group. Or they may relate to the practice of a particular profession, to its ethos or professional ethic. Just as an individual practitioner would feel bound, as a Christian, to maintain the ethics of his profession and to submit them to criticism, so he would think it appropriate for the Church to assist in this process; and practitioners and laymen who were not committed Christians would, for the most part, accept and even welcome the contribution of the Church so long as it is serious and informed.

There is an assumption underlying all this which requires to be made explicit. It is that the standards observed in this country are, if not distinctively Christian, at least a reasonable approximation to what Christianity demands, so that the Church in acknowledging a responsibility for them, even though it is a critical one, is not compromising its Christian witness. There are those who would challenge this – who, while conceding for the most part that those active in public life and in the central institutions of our society are upright men and women doing their duty as they see it, would claim, nevertheless, that the entire fabric is based on a degree of social injustice which fatally vitiates their activities and attitudes, as in the case of the Indian civil servant.

To the extent that this critique of the *status quo* is advanced, the area of political controversy (in the party political sense) threatens to expand into the entire political arena. Hence, to conclude that there are fairly wide areas about which the Church has by common consent a right and a duty to pronounce is something one is entitled to do (if at all) only after an examination of the role (if any) of the Church in party political controversy.

It is sometimes suggested that political differences (in this sense of 'political') are differences about means, whereas Christian theology is concerned with ends. Christian Conservatives and Christian Socialists can agree about the latter, while disagreeing about the former. But neither limb of this dichotomy is true. Conservatives and Socialists do, indeed, differ *inter alia* as to whether, for example, increased public investment or encouragement of market forces together with strict fiscal policy will be most likely to reduce unemployment, both parties wanting to reduce unemployment; but they also differ as to the sort of society they want to see. Not only do they differ as to the balance to be sought between values which they both acknowledge, they differ as to these values themselves. Socialists are prepared to agree that a balance needs to be kept between the demands of equality and those of liberty, and they tend, in cases of severe conflict, to give those of equality the greater weight. Conservatives not only prize liberty more highly; they doubt the claims of equality altogether. A typical Conservative position would be that social policy should be determined by justice and by humanity, and that neither of these implies equality. There are deep philosophical questions at issue here and they are questions about ends.

Similarly, moral theology is not concerned only about ends, as the debate about nuclear weapons clearly indicates. It is not just a matter of both parties to the theological debate sharing a desire for peace but differing about how to achieve it. There is disagreement as to the moral legitimacy of a threat to use nuclear weapons.

This being so, it is evident that the Church faces a dilemma.

The domain of party politics covers a great deal of our social and political life, on any showing, and there are some standpoints from which it covers virtually all of it. For the Church to acknowledge a responsibility for politics and to claim that Christian doctrine has political implications while keeping entirely clear of the party political domain, is to render her witness limited and ineffective. Yet on these issues the Church's membership is deeply divided, and the Church has a duty to give spiritual comfort and succour to all her members. It is not simply that there are Christians who are Socialists and Christians who are Conservatives. There are Christians who endeavour to discharge their Christian duty through an active career as Socialist politicians or party workers, and other Christians who are similarly active in politics as Conservatives. It is not just that they feel that they should bring their Christianity to bear upon their political life; they choose that mode of political activity, in part at least, out of Christian conviction.

There are various possible ways of resolving the dilemma.

1. One way would be to argue that, if Christianity has political implications, it ought to be evident what these are. So, if Christians disagree politically and both sides cannot be right, the individual who is committed politically is bound to stigmatise his opponents not only as mistaken but also as unchristian. They have failed to see the light or failed to follow it. A Christian who was properly instructed theologically and understood the political issues could not be a Conservative (or a Socialist). That many claim to be both Christian and Conservative (or Socialist) is due to a failure of insight into the true political implications of Christianity, which failure requires to be explained (with all due charity) in terms of social and historical influences of a subtly corrupting kind.

2. If this seems implausible, given the outstanding integrity and good sense of some Socialists and Conservatives, and the depth and sincerity of their Christian commitment, it may be tempting to withdraw to the conception of Christian faith as a sort of spiritual essence that can be made to inform any sort of

politics, whatever its character. But it is evident that there are political regimes and political philosophies which are manifestly incompatible with Christian belief and which Christians of all parties would be bound to repudiate.

3. A further possibility is to argue that there are, as it happens, good Christian reasons for being a Socialist and good Christian reasons also for being a Conservative; that both positions represent attempts to reconcile important Christian values in the face of the inevitable uncertainties and ambiguities of politics, attempts which are necessarily imperfect and, to a certain extent, incommensurable.

There are aspects, in particular, of the division between Right and Left, which support this suggestion. The vision of the Left has been one of a realisation of the kingdom of God on earth. The emphasis has been on an ideal state of affairs, to be worked for now, in which the relations between men in a total society should be free and equal and co-operative, as they can be sometimes in small face-to-face communities. By comparison with this ideal any existing political entity is inevitably found wanting. The theological inspiration of this vision is evident (even in its Marxist version). The Right, by contrast, has concentrated on 'political realities', on the inevitable limitations of political action and the corruptions attendant upon the exercise of political power. There are elements in the Christian tradition which support each of the contending political movements, and they are elements, moreover, which neither party can entirely discount.

The other respect in which Right and Left disagree reflects a much more general division, to be found in theology as elsewhere, between conservatives and radicals. In any society there is a tension between those whose primary concern is to conserve what is good at the cost, if necessary, of keeping some things that are bad, and those who are most concerned to destroy what is bad at the cost, if necessary, of losing some things that are good. These attitudes owe something to the temperament of individuals, but something also to their oc-cupation and social status. Lord Devlin has argued, for in-stance, that the judiciary, and the legal profession generally, both are and ought to be conservative. Their primary role is to defend the rights and liberties we at present enjoy; it is for others to inaugurate changes. If Devlin is right the bench will tend to attract conservatively minded persons 'with a stake in the country', and there is nothing wrong in this. Social workers, on the other hand, observe at first hand the disadvantages suffered by those who are least well off, and the concern for their welfare which animates their professional vocation leads naturally to a demand for political action to improve their lot. Of course the Left is not always radical in tendency or the Right conservative – the trade unions are, in many respects, conservative bodies and the Institute of Directors can be radical – but, broadly speaking, political divisions do reflect this universal tension between those who favour change and those who wish to preserve the *status quo*. These contrasting attitudes are liable, in the Church as elsewhere, to be infected with sin, although conservatives and radicals are tempted to different sins. On the whole the sin of the Right is complacency, the sin of the Left self-righteousness.

If, then, there is substantial theological support for, broadly, Conservative and Socialist political philosophies, and if they reflect enduring differences of temperament and political emphasis, it is implausible to suggest that the dilemma posed to the Church by the existence of these opposing tendencies can be resolved by concluding that one or other of them alone is what follows unambiguously from a true interpretation of the Christian faith.

If this is so, it provides, incidentally, an argument for an accepted party system in which the philosophies and the programmes of the various parties are exposed to the criticisms of their opponents and to the judgement of a population at large which is not finally committed to any of them. Given the partisan pressures in such a system which to some extent inevitably restrict the vision of politicians, it is just as well that plenty of people, including many convinced Christians, are not politically active.

But it may still be felt that insufficient account has been taken of the threat to the unity of the Church if it becomes at all involved in politics. We ought to remember how many and how serious are the factors that intensify political divisions. Those on opposite sides of the political divide will tend to move in different circles, read different newspapers, find their allies in different sectors of secular thought and action, and employ, as time goes on, increasingly divergent vocabularies. And these differences will tend to work their way back into theology to produce the situation which exercises Norman, in which Christianity is, or appears to be, reduced to politics or, at least, comes to be interpreted in terms of certain political categories. Thus someone who begins by supporting the Left in politics through a generous and Christianly motivated desire to serve the oppressed may find his most effective allies among Marxists and, through dialogue with Marxists, he may come to stress those elements in Christianity which are most conformable to Marxism. On the other hand, someone who begins by inclining to the Right through the conviction that the pervasive influence of sin allows only for piecemeal and pragmatic ventures in politics may find himself involved with people whose distrust of abstract principle and attachment to the existing distribution of power is less disinterested than his own. He will be strongly tempted to justify an increasingly unprincipled pragmatism by stressing unduly the other-worldly elements in the gospel.

It cannot be denied that these are real dangers, but we must be careful not to overlook the divisions which, already and inevitably, exist in the Church. As Peter Hinchliff has pointed out, the Church is itself, *inter alia*, a political institution with its own parties and 'Church politics', and, although these do not correspond entirely to the divisions of national politics, there is also to be found in them a broad distinction between conservative and radical. The case for keeping the Church out of politics, in so far as it rests upon a desire to avoid dissension, is weakened by the existence of Church politics. Indeed divisions in the Church might well be judged less distressing to the degree that they are not entirely introverted. One political question which the Church as an institution cannot avoid is that of the proper relationship between Church and state;

and, if this is taken seriously, wider political questions are bound to arise. Does its establishment make the Church part of 'the Establishment', and is this compatible with its mission to the poor and the outcast? Is ours a 'plural society', and, if so, should the Church of England, and indeed the Christian religion, occupy a privileged status? What is, or should be, the relationship between the Church and culture? Should the Church acknowledge an obligation to the whole nation, even at the risk of condoning in practice much that is doubtfully or marginally Christian? Or should it content itself with ministering to gathered congregations who may be presumed to be more purely and thoroughly committed?

There are sharp differences of opinion on these issues which sometimes reflect and sometimes cut across broader political divisions in the life of the country and cannot be reasonably considered in isolation from them.

It is often complained that there is too little appeal to fundamental theology in the way the Church reaches decisions about its own internal problems, let alone those of society at large. And this may well be true. But appeal to doctrine is itself not guaranteed to yield agreement. There are doctrinal disagreements also in the Church, and these are not wholly unrelated to or unaffected by the political differences they are invoked to resolve. In particular the radical/conservative axis is as conspicuous in theology as it is in politics. I do not see how this interaction can be denied or repudiated, although it is open to the distortions of which Norman and others have complained.

If, then, the question is asked how far the Church as an institution should concern itself with political issues, the following answers suggest themselves.

1. The Church has no alternative but to make up its mind on those political questions which concern its own status in relation to the state and society, and any serious attempt to resolve these problems will involve some of the broader issues in political philosophy which divide the political parties. The Church is not likely to conduct these discussions well unless there is a continuing theological debate in which they are

regularly considered. It is not to be expected that the divergent opinions within the Church about these matters will be entirely reconciled, any more than they are in national politics, and the best that can be achieved will often be a compromise.

2. Individual Christians who are active in politics, or even simply in the various roles that go to make up social life, may reasonably expect the Church to help them clarify and purify their 'operative ideals' and enable them to recognise the moral costs and moral opportunities of what they are doing or trying to do. Since effective action of a broadly political kind always involves compromise, it is important to be clear-sighted as to what the underlying principles are and to what extent, and for what reason, they are being overridden.

3. There are times when the Church as an institution must condemn flagrant and wanton cruelty and injustice, and the claims of political movements to encompass the whole of human life. It is such idolatrous claims, not a secular provenance as such, which render a political system unacceptable to Christians.

4. Though Christian faith has implications for political thought and action, it is not exhausted by them or even adequately exhibited in them. Though charity and forgiveness in face-to-face relations are not all that the Christian is called to, they lie at the heart of the Christian faith, and political improvement without them is nothing worth.

6

'INDOCTRINATION'*

The word 'indoctrination' has strong pejorative force, and its use belongs most naturally to the realm of polemics. In a reasoned treatment of religious education one would like for that reason to avoid it. Nevertheless, it does draw attention to a genuine problem, which needs to be faced. The charge is often made that religious education involves 'indoctrination', and that this is enough to condemn it. In reply it is often argued that religious education need not and should not involve 'indoctrination'. Can we do anything to clarify this controversy?

It is, as we have remarked, the critic of religious education who tends to introduce the word into the discussion. For him it means the inculcation of (especially religious) doctrines in a manner that is objectionable. The problem for him is to specify more precisely *what* it is that he feels to be objectionable. In the literature attempts have been made to locate this in (1) a certain *method* of teaching; (2) a certain *content* of teaching; (3) a certain *aim* in teaching.

Method

In this sense A indoctrinates B in respect of *p* (a belief) if A brings it about that B believes *p* otherwise than by enabling B to understand the reasons for *p*. Indoctrination in this sense is unavoidable. Every teacher, at every stage in the educational

*From *The Fourth R, the Durham Report on Religious Education* (London: SPCK, 1970), pp. 353–8.

process, with every subject, has to some extent to 'indoctrinate' his pupils. No one can always produce sufficient reasons for every statement he gets others to believe – (1) because they cannot always understand the reasons; (2) because he does not always know the reasons; he himself accepts a good deal on authority; (3) because life is too short. As Willis Moore writes,

> What I propose . . . is that we frankly admit that learning necessarily begins with an authoritative and indoctrinative situation, and that for lack of time, native capacity or the requisite training to think everything out for oneself, learning even for the rationally mature individual must continue to include an ingredient of the unreasoned, the merely accepted. The extent to which every one of us must depend, and wisely so, on the authoritative pronouncements of those who are more expert than are we in most of the problems we face is evidence enough of the truth of this contention. It would seem to be more in accord with reality to consider the 'indoctrination' and the 'education' of the earlier liberal educators to be the polar extremes of a continuum of teaching method along which actual teaching may move in keeping with the requirements of the situation. With infants in nearly everything and with mature, reasoning adults in very little, the teacher will use indoctrinating procedures. Between the two extremes the proper mixture of the one method with the other is appropriately determined by the degree of rational capability of the learner with regard to the subject matter before him and the degree of urgency of the situation.[1]

Since it is impossible to dispense with indoctrination conceived merely as a method, the critic of indoctrination (who wishes the word, so far as possible, to have pejorative force in all contexts) proceeds to introduce some limitation as to *content*.

Content

In this sense A indoctrinates B in respect of *p* if A brings it about that B believes *p* otherwise than by enabling B to understand the reasons for *p*; *where* p *is a debatable or controversial statement.* The objection now is to 'teaching of reasonably disputatious doctrines as if they were known facts'.[2] Flew argues that the right way to meet Moore's point is by introducing into the concept of indoctrination some appropriate essential references to content;

> or, as the case may be, by recognizing that these are already there . . . The notion must be limited first to the presentation of debatable issues; and then further perhaps to the would-be factual, as opposed to the purely normative. Once some such limitation, or limitations, have been made it ceases to be necessary to allow that any indoctrination at all is 'inevitable'.

Flew's inclination to exclude 'the purely normative' is presumably due to his recognising the force of the argument that some 'norms' at least must be accepted by the child before he is capable of understanding the reasons for them. Flew's argument assumes (1) that it is possible to delimit the class of 'controversial' or 'debatable' would-be actual beliefs and (2) that it is never necessary to use 'indoctrinatory procedures' (as set out in 'Method' above) in respect of them. With respect to (1) how is this requirement to be satisfied? We might say (a) that a belief *p* is 'controversial' if it is possible for a reasonable man to believe not-*p*. This would seem to be much too wide. There must be very few serious opinions which have not, at some time or other, somewhere or other, been held by reasonable men. We might amend this to (b) '. . . if there are today reasonable and reasonably well-informed men who believe not-*p*'. This might do and should not be too difficult to apply. Flew might think it still too wide, and there are indications that he is looking for a different *sort* of distinction. 'For surely, we cannot out of hand dismiss basic differences of *logical status* [my italics] in the content of what is taught as irrelevant to the question of how, if at all, these different sorts of thing ought to be taught.' This suggests that, perhaps, for example, historical questions are not, in his sense, 'debatable', although they do provoke a great deal of debate, while religious or 'metaphysical' questions are. So perhaps we might try, instead of (b), (c) '. . . if it belongs to a class of beliefs whose logical status renders them (in some way to be elucidated) essentially controversial'. It is not at all clear that one can, in the way proposed, draw a clear line between, for example, history and metaphysics, and Flew has not done it for us, but I propose to try out both definitions (b) and (c) in relation to (2) – whether one can altogether avoid 'indoctrinatory procedures' in respect of them.

Willis Moore in his article seeks to distinguish between 'education' and 'indoctrination'. He makes the illuminating point that:

> The supporting philosophies of man whence flow these two methods of teaching provide the basic distinction we seek. The liberal believes in a latent rationality in every normal infant, a capacity for reasoned decision-making that, under careful cultivation and through practice, can be enhanced and developed. The authoritarian holds that the vast majority of mankind remain indefinitely juvenile in their responses, hence indefinitely in need of restrictive guidance and management in all important areas of behaviour. *Most liberals feel, however, that man is innately either biased in favour of the good and the right or, at worst, neutral with respect to them* [my italics]. The authoritarian suspects man of a bias in favour of the evil and wrong or that he is possessed of an original sin from which only a miracle can save him. The difference between the two philosophies and consequent methods of teaching should be seen not as the absolute white versus black of the older liberalism but as one of degree only, yet a very significant degree.

There can be no doubt, I think, that this liberal 'philosophy' (as Moore significantly terms it) is 'controversial' according to both definitions (b) and (c). There are reasonable men who do not accept it and it has a 'metaphysical' character. It is, or is part of, a 'philosophy of life'.

The first thing to notice, then, is that the entire *liberal approach to education* (let alone the particular methods its protagonists choose to employ) depends on a 'controversial' or 'debatable' position. So equally does the authoritarian approach. But the relevant question for our present purpose is 'Can or should the liberal refrain altogether from using "indoctrinatory procedures" in conveying this liberal attitude to his pupils?' Must he refrain from doing anything, whether by word or example, to bring it about that a child believes that other children in the school are 'innately biased in favour of the good', without at the same time providing the child with evidence sufficient to convince a reasonable man of the truth of this controversial proposition? If Johnny is being consistently beastly to Tommy and Tommy is tempted to condemn Johnny out of hand, must the teacher avoid saying anything like 'Johnny is really good at heart' because he cannot there and then convince Tommy by rational means of the truth of this apparently implausible and certainly disputable assertion? It seems to me perfectly clear that the liberal teacher in a liberal school will do everything in his power to communicate by persuasion, by his own personal example and by choice of other exemplars, indeed by the whole ethos of the school, this liberal attitude. He will, of course, endeavour, as soon as it is possible and so far as it is possible, to enable the child to see for himself how and why men are basically good, *etc.*, but unless he has devised an environment in which 'actions speak louder than words' he is going to find this difficult or impossible. The liberal is likely also to be a believer in democracy, and he will presumably presuppose in his ordering of the school, and teach by word and example, *etc.*, those fundamental beliefs about human beings (their rationality, their need to participate in decisions affecting themselves) upon which democratic institutions rest, beliefs which are certainly 'controversial' and which he can only adequately justify at a comparatively late stage in the educational process.

Flew resists this conclusion:

Even if it were the case – and I do not myself admit that even this is proved – that democratic institutions somehow presuppose the general acceptance of some similarly disputatious would-be factual beliefs, it still would not follow that it is in the interests of such deservedly cherished institutions either necessary or prudent to indoctrinate our children with these congenial beliefs.

We might consistently and properly insist, with Dewey and his followers, that 'The means is constitutive with respect to the end: authoritarian methods tend to create authoritarian products . . .'

It seems to me that Flew is here confronted by a dilemma. He can *either* refuse to adopt *any* 'indoctrinatory procedures', like the more extreme liberals who, as Moore puts it, 'took the bull by the horns by advocating a nearly total permissiveness in the earliest learning situations, thus eliminating indoctrination in teaching by doing away with teaching'; *or* deliberately attempt by manipulating the child's environment in different ways to induce in him attitudes and beliefs favourable to democracy. If he adopts the former policy, it is highly improbable that he will succeed in producing the sort of democratic personality he wishes; if the latter, he is engaged in indoctrination as he has defined it.

It is at this point that I might usefully turn to the definition of indoctrination in terms of *aims*, as well as *method* and *content*.

Aims

The suggestion now is that 'A indoctrinates B in respect of p, if he brings it about or seeks to bring it about that B believes p in such a way that he is unable subsequently to believe not-p.' In order not to convict of indoctrination the teacher who produces in his pupils an unalterable conviction that $2 + 2 = 4$, we should perhaps add 'even if presented with sufficient reasons for believing not-*p*'. In other words, to indoctrinate with respect to *p* is to produce an entirely closed mind with respect to *p*. Something of this sort is probably what many people have in mind when they object to 'indoctrination'. 'Indoctrination' of this extreme kind is, alas, not unknown in religious education, but the most conspicuous contemporary examples are to be found among fanatical nationalists or communists. We could, of course, regard as 'indoctrination' an educational process whose aims are less extreme than this, not to make it impossible, but merely more or less difficult for the individual to change his mind if given good reason; which aims to give him a permanent *bias* in a particular direction.

If we do relax the definition in this way, can we still condemn 'indoctrination' unreservedly? This may well depend on where we find ourselves along the liberal–authoritarian axis. The liberal aims at enabling the individual to realise his potentialities as a rational, autonomous adult. He will use indoctrinatory procedures as little as he can and he will regard his teaching as successful to the extent that his pupil comes to think entirely for himself. He is confident that, when this happens, his pupil will be as well equipped as anyone else to make wise decisions.

An educator will tend to move away from the liberal towards the authoritarian pole of the axis to the extent that he doubts the possibility or the desirability of the liberal's aim. 'The authoritarian,' says Moore, 'holds that the vast majority of mankind remain indefinitely juvenile in their responses, hence indefinitely in need of restrictive guidance and management in all important areas of behaviour.' In other words, the authoritarian doubts whether people who think for themselves will necessarily think for the best. The classical exponent of the extreme form of this position is Plato, whose philosopher-kings would select those capable of 'education' and 'indoctrinate' the rest. It can safely be said that none of our own contemporary educators would take such an extreme position seriously. A more powerful challenge to the extreme liberal view is that of Burke, when he recommends adherence to 'prejudice with the reason involved', rather than relying simply on 'the naked reason', because

> prejudice with its reason, has a motive to give action to that reason, and an affection that will give it permanence. Prejudice is of ready application in the emergency; it previously engages the mind in a steady course of wisdom and virtue, and does not leave the man hesitating in the moment of decision, sceptical, puzzled, and unresolved. Prejudice renders a man's virtue his habit; and not a series of unconnected acts. Through just prejudice, his duty becomes a part of his nature.[3]

Burke's argument may be developed as follows.

1. The liberal ideal of the wholly autonomous rational individual subjecting all his beliefs to criticism and retaining only those that survive the test cannot be realised. Every individual grows to maturity in a cultural tradition and cannot produce a rational 'philosophy' of his own from scratch.

2. It is not only false but dangerous for the individual to *think* he is capable of doing this. Society depends for its proper functioning upon a multiplicity of shared beliefs, values, and attitudes, and will suffer to an indefinite extent if the individual feels that these have no claim upon him except in so far as he can independently validate them.

3. To the extent that these shared beliefs, *etc.*, are eroded by 'rational' criticism, their place in the life of the individual and society will be taken not by beliefs, values, and attitudes that are (for the first time) based on good reasons, but by ideas that are largely the product of current fashions. Educators who scrupulously refrain from introducing any bias into the educational process will not thereby ensure that their pupils escape bias, only that the bias is imparted by other agencies.

In the light of this discussion it would appear that neither the extreme liberal nor the extreme authoritarian thesis is at all plausible and that the sensible educator will take up some sort of intermediate position. He will not use 'indoctrinatory procedures' more than is necessary (and he will always respect the personality of the pupil), but he will not feel guilty about using them when they *are* necessary. He will not expect or intend to produce an educated adult who has no beliefs, values or attitudes which he cannot rationally defend against all comers and who is incapable of settled convictions, deep-seated virtues or profound loyalties. But neither will he treat his pupils in such a way as to leave them with closed minds and restricted sympathies. The process of being educated is like learning to build a house by actually building one and then having to live in the house one has built. It is a process in which the individual inevitably requires help. The extreme authoritarian helps by building the house himself, according to what he believes to be the best plan, and making the novice live in it. He designs it in such a way as to make it as difficult as possible for the novice to alter it. The extreme liberal leaves the novice to find his own materials and devise his own plan, for fear of exercising improper influence. The most he will do is provide strictly technical information if asked. The sensible educator helps the novice to build the best house he can (in the light of accumulated experience). He strikes a balance between the need to produce a good house and the desirability of letting the novice make his own choices; but he is careful that the house is designed in such a way that it can subsequently be altered and improved as the owner, no longer a novice, sees fit.

This analogy is simply an elaboration of Aristotle's remark that 'men become lyre-players by playing the lyre, house-builders by building houses and just men by performing just actions'.[4] Aristotle saw the need for the individual to grow into a desirable pattern of intellectual and moral dispositions whose rational basis he learns as he develops, but could not learn unless the underlying dispositions were already there. Aristotle, no doubt, makes too little provision for originality. This defect is made good by Gilbert Murray's comment on Euripides: 'Every man who possesses real vitality can be seen as the resultant of two forces. He is first the child of a particular . . . tradition. He is secondly, in one degree or another, a rebel against that tradition. And the best traditions make the best rebels.'[5] The liberal wants to make sure that we produce rebels; the authoritarian that we do not produce rebels. The sensible educator is concerned to produce good rebels.

7

REASON AND COMMITMENT IN THE ACADEMIC VOCATION*

I have experienced two emotions in the course of our various conferences. One – the predominant one – is excitement at the discovery that colleagues in other subjects and in other universities have been troubled by the same disquiet as myself about the way in which academic work is understood and practised, and are formulating their problems in much the same way as I have been trying to do; the other is bewilderment at the complexity of the problems as soon as one tries to get them clear.

Perhaps, then, it will help if I start from a very simple position which I should have regarded as a gross caricature if I had not heard it enunciated by more than one eminent scientist at a conference I recently attended. According to this view the academic should aim at objectivity, and objectivity is attainable only in science. Outside science there is only the realm of subjective opinion, characterised dismissively as 'poetry'. *Prima facie* this position excludes from the academic community all those who practise arts subjects, but room may be found for those who practise them in a scientific way. What precisely this involves is not usually specified, but characteristically the use of symbolic notations, operational definitions and precise measurement is regarded as indicative of a scientific approach. The task of delimiting the boundaries of science has proved enormously difficult, and it would be a

* Originally read to a conference on 'The Academic Vocation' organised by the University Teachers Group, Oxford, 1975. From the *Oxford Review of Education* 2 (1976), pp. 101–109.

bold philosopher who claimed that it had been satisfactorily accomplished. Nevertheless the attempt to do so has for some time put the humanities on the defensive, and this is one reason why one encounters very often in arts faculties a tendency to accord greater prestige to those aspects of a subject which are 'tough' and 'rigorous', such as, in the study of languages, linguistics, in philosophy, formal logic, in theology, gospel criticism. Whether or not these can be regarded as strictly scientific, they resemble science in being susceptible of comparatively precise formulation and, given certain assumptions, an agreed decision-procedure. Maurice Broady hits it off well when he refers to 'operations of a fairly technical kind by which we come to a decision'.[1]

This tendency deserves to be examined with some care, for it extends far beyond the naive dogmatism of certain natural scientists philosophising outside their own subject. We are all to some extent affected by it, when we warn our pupils against 'soft options' or endeavour to keep them out of the syllabus altogether, when we advise on suitable thesis topics, or establish priorities for chairs. A tendency so widespread is unlikely to be altogether mistaken, and we need to do justice to its merits before we stress its limitations.

Its chief merit, I suggest, is this. We are by nature intellectually lazy. Left to ourselves, we find it comfortable to be ruled by prejudice or by prevailing fashions. To be an academic at all is to think it possible that one may be mistaken, and the easiest way to be mistaken is not to take the trouble to think, or to think only in a manner that offers the subjective experience of intellectual activity without the shock of correction. Thought is enjoyed as an agreeable form of self-expression. To combat this native vice requires an early and insistent emphasis upon *rigour*; upon clarity of expression, upon recognition of and search for unwelcome facts, and upon the use of any methods that will correct individual bias. Thus where strictly scientific techniques are available and appropriate they should be used, and in arts subjects, where there may be no techniques which are strictly scientific, precise definition, accurate analysis and patient accumulation of evidence should be demanded. Students are often hostile to this demand. The requirement that they should submit assertions to detailed analysis and subject themselves to an 'impersonal' technique is felt to be an unwarranted limitation upon their autonomy. How often have I interviewed undergraduates wishing to change their subject in order the more truly to express themselves, and how often have I had to tell them that philosophy too has its technical requirements which they will have to master before they are able to develop their views about the meaning of life! So the claims of objectivity, as Maurice Broady understands them, are not to be denied. And, as university teachers, we are, I believe, under an obligation to ensure, so far as we can, that they are given due respect throughout our educational system.

But there is a constant temptation to go further and to maintain one or other or both of two positions which are not justified; *viz.*, to hold either (1) that only those questions are genuine questions which can be handled by these 'objective' methods; or (2) that only such questions are capable of rational discussion. It is often the explicit or implicit acceptance of these positions on the part of their teachers which leads students to reject 'objectivity' as such.

All of us will be able to provide illustrations of these trends, such as the persistent vogue of behaviourism in psychology, the reluctance of historians to venture upon the history of ideas, the neglect by economists of non-quantifiable elements in welfare.

These trends are only partly explained by the prestige of science. Sometimes, indeed, the choice of what shall constitute the 'rigorous core' of a subject is determinedly non-scientific, as happens in the case of history. Attempts at abstraction and generalisation are resisted by historians in favour of the patient accumulation of facts; and 'scientific history' is scientific not in virtue of taking over the methods of natural science, but in virtue of applying its own independent standards of rigour. The same would be true of linguistic philosophy in relation to the scientific study of language.

Natural science, then, may be the paradigm case of rigour, but the practitioners of each discipline are jealous of whatever is peculiar to that discipline and tend to interpret 'rigour' accordingly.

Aristotle maintained that only such a degree of precision should be sought in any study as is appropriate to that study and this principle deserves to be kept steadily in mind. When it is not, the following evils develop.

1. Questionable assumptions go unquestioned. I said earlier, in characterising 'objectivity', that objectivity allows of 'comparatively precise formulation and, given certain assumptions, an agreed decision-procedure.' It is these assumptions which the purely 'objective' scholar tends to overlook, either because they are not themselves suitable for rigorous treatment, or because he has no time to subject them to such treatment, or because the rigorous treatment that would be appropriate belongs to some other discipline.

2. Transdisciplinary problems go unnoticed or, at least, unexplored, for the task of exploring them, *ex hypothesi*, cannot be discharged, at least initially, with the desired rigour. Hence a recent reviewer referred, with understandable fastidiousness, to 'the *ooze* of interdisciplinary studies'. A constant complaint – and a justified one – of students reading combined courses is that nothing much is done to relate the various subjects to one another; and the reason is that this relating is not itself a subject. No one is an expert in it. I have not forgotten the experience of listening to a social psychologist and a sociologist, in an interdisciplinary group, discussing the 'interface' between their two subjects, and my own astonishment that they did not know what was going on in each other's field although, as became increasingly evident, (a) any balanced understanding of society must include both, (b) each, for its own proper development, needs to be complemented by the other.

3. Metaphysical questions are either neglected altogether or discussed at a level of abstraction which removes them from serious empirical testing and encourages the impression that no such testing is possible or necessary.

The tendency of academics to concentrate their attention upon those areas that can be treated 'objectively', though it starts from a sound instinct as to what is essential to scholarship of any kind, easily develops into the very avoidance of thinking which it was designed to correct. For when someone has become expert at handling a technique, he achieves a peculiar satisfaction from it and a certain prestige; not only is it uncomfortable to question the underlying assumptions, but it requires him to venture upon territory in which he has no assured mastery and which in all likelihood is not capable of being mastered in the manner he is used to. J. L. Austin used to refer to the sensation of alarm 'when the firm ground of prejudice begins to give way beneath one's feet', and this sensation is bound to attend anyone who ventures upon 'the ooze of interdisciplinary studies'. It is not surprising, therefore, that academics, having surmounted all the obstacles on the hard and stony track towards some modest pinnacle of competence, tend to make a virtue of staying there rather than set out into the surrounding bog. Particularly as they suspect, with some reason, that their pupils prefer the bog precisely because it largely cancels the advantages of the skilled mountaineer and brings teacher and taught into greater equality. Moreover the area is the favourite terrain of publicists, journalists and pundits of every kind, whom most academics view with profound distrust – and very often rightly.

This account is exaggerated. I am talking of tendencies; and most academics, while aware of the tendencies I have mentioned, realise that much of their work is, and will remain, controversial; that it calls for trained judgement and lacks an agreed decision-procedure. The literary critic, the historian, the philosopher generally recognises that he is comparatively rarely in a position to show by 'operations of a fairly technical kind' that his opponent is wrong or even to measure at all precisely the probability that he is. Even in natural science, where 'objectivity' of this kind is most at home, there are decisions to be taken as to which of a number of rival theories shall be chosen, when each can more or less account for the facts. These decisions call for the scientist's judgement of such considerations as simplicity, scope, fruitfulness, coherence, elegance. That the making of these choices is not reducible to a technique is well put by T. S. Kuhn:

> What I am denying then is neither the existence of good reasons nor that these reasons are of the sort usually described. I am, however, insisting that such reasons constitute values to be used in making choices rather than rules of choice . . . Simplicity, scope, fruitfulness and even accuracy can be judged quite differently (which is not to say that they may be judged arbitrarily) by different people. Again they may differ in their conclusions without violating any accepted rule.[2]

Hence the scientists with whom I started, who dismissed all non-science as poetry, were being unduly naive even about the rational structure of science itself. It is not only in interdisciplinary studies, let alone in metaphysical enquiry, that 'objectivity' is not enough. There is an irreducible element of personal judgement in all, or almost all, academic work. (The hesitation concerns mathematics, about which I know too little even to hazard a guess, though colleagues tell me that here too a great deal turns on individual decision.)

As soon as this is recognised the problem of impartiality arises. Wherever a question is susceptible of 'objective treatment' (*i.e.* wherever an agreed decision-procedure exists) one has a duty to be 'objective', but once the bounds of 'objectivity' are passed, the questions are, *ex hypothesi*, to a greater or lesser extent controversial. In Kuhn's words they 'can be judged quite differently (which is not to say that they may be judged arbitrarily) by different people'.

To take an example. There is a notorious problem in the interpretation of Plato's *Republic*. Plato recognises, or appears to recognise, four levels of cognition, ranging from conjecture to knowledge, and illustrates this scheme by a diagram of a line unequally divided, with each of the two sections thus produced divided again in the same proportion. He then goes on to tell[3] a dramatic story of prisoners condemned to live in a cave watching shadows until one of them manages to escape and finds his way out of the cave into the sunlight. Plato stresses the reluctance of the released prisoner, at every stage of his journey, to shift his gaze from shadow to reality, from darkness to light. The disputed question is whether Plato intended the Cave to exhibit in allegorised form the stages set out in the Line (and what, in any case, these stages are). Scholars have differed, and still differ, in their answers to this question. It clearly cannot be settled by 'operations of a fairly technical kind', though strict standards of scholarship require to be observed. As it so happens, I believe that I have the solution to this problem; that is to say, that I can offer an interpretation of the whole sequence which makes better sense than any alternative on offer. There are certain passages, which are to my mind of obvious centrality and importance, whose sense is comparatively plain and which afford the clue to Plato's meaning. There are, I concede, certain other passages (less central and less important, as I think), which *prima facie* conflict with my interpretation, but I believe that I can show that these discrepant passages can be understood in a way that is consistent with it, and that, so understood, they actually gain in intelligibility.

Here, then, is a fairly typical situation in the humanities (and, I should guess, in the sciences as well). When taking students through this part of Plato, should I be impartial, and what does impartiality require?

Well, what am I trying to do? I am trying to help them understand Plato's thought and I am also trying to teach them how to interpret a text and how to think philosophically. It might seem that the first aim could be achieved (given my confidence in the rightness of my own interpretation) by simply telling them that Plato means what I personally believe him to mean. But that way they will not learn how I came to form my opinion, so they will learn nothing about the problems of interpreting a text; nor, since this is a philosophical text, will they learn much about the nature of philosophical thinking. Moreover, the merit of my own interpretation consists precisely in the success with which it resolves apparent inconsistencies in the original, and they will not fully understand Plato's meaning in this particular sequence (even on the assumption that I am right about it) unless they appreciate those features of it which appear at least to suggest alternative interpretations. So that I am bound to place before them, so far as I am able, the main alternatives to my own interpretation, and explain, in relation to the text, why I do not accept them.

Now it may be objected that, if I proceed in this way, I am not being entirely impartial, because I do communicate to them my own conclusions, and, in so doing, lend those conclusions whatever authority I may possess. What I ought really to do, it may be said, is set out the arguments pro and con and leave the students to decide for themselves what is the proper conclusion. In other words I ought to be neutral as between conflicting interpretations. There are three points to make about this.

1. As a method it is sometimes appropriate; it forces the student to make up his own mind. But if universally adopted it would encourage the view, quite commonly held as it is, that the proper scholarly attitude is suspense of judgement. And this is a mistake; the good scholar is not one who refuses to judge, but one who judges reasonably in the light of the available evidence; and no one will ever learn to do this who does not have the opportunity of discovering how mature scholars do it.

2. Neutrality of this kind is to be distinguished from impartiality and is not implied by it. Impartiality requires, not that I refrain from reaching a conclusion about the interpretation of Plato, but that I am fair to the arguments of my opponents; that I do not misrepresent their substance or underestimate their weight.

3. Impartiality, as distinct from neutrality, presupposes some standard of judgement which is to be respected. Partiality involves favouring one party in a dispute to a greater extent than the justice of his cause deserves, whereas neutrality means simply favouring neither party. This is why the

concept of impartiality has its place only in relation to disputes which are in principle open to rational decision.

What I have been saying so far is extremely trite. I have deliberately taken a rather routine example, because in discussions of this sort one so easily becomes lost in abstractions. However, it may well be objected that my example avoids all the difficulties. Philosophical scholarship, particularly when exercised on a thinker remote from us in time, does not engage the passions in such a way as seriously to threaten impartiality, and does not readily arouse doubts as to the very possibility of it. Of these objections the second is manifestly the more important. But something should be said about the first. Only someone ignorant of the psychology of academics could believe that among them prejudice and passion are confined to what is of obvious, universal and immediate importance. Indeed my own observations suggest that the bitterest feuds and the most unbridled fury are provoked by the most austerely academic topics. Philosophical conferences rarely witness savage encounters in the philosophy of religion, political philosophy or moral philosophy; but comparatively often in the fields of logic and epistemology. The reasons for this are implicit in the earlier part of my paper. It is in the 'rigorous core' of a subject that the academic's *amour-propre* is ordinarily vested. And perhaps it is also true that it is those subjects which are most nearly susceptible of wholly 'objective' treatment, that, because they arouse the liveliest expectation of agreement, engender the greatest frustration when this is not readily achieved. It is very tempting in such cases to attribute the failure to agree to the perversity and obstinate wrongheadedness of one's opponents. Nevertheless this phenomenon need not worry us greatly. We can see how the temptation to partiality arises in such contexts, but we also recognise that it can and should be resisted.

(Or should it entirely? It may be that the obsessive partisanship of at any rate some scholars does contribute to the optimum development of rival theories and the elimination of the less defensible; though it has also to be said that all sorts of non-rational devices are often employed with rather little scruple in these encounters, which [the cliché is significant] 'generate more heat than light'.)

The serious doubts begin to arise when we consider large-scale differences of approach, like that between the schools of sociology that Maurice Broady mentioned. As he explained the points at issue between these schools, the main question was whether sociology can be objective (as the one school maintained), or whether (as the other held), it necessarily reflects the interests of society and cannot, therefore, be value-free. The implication was, I think, that if the latter school were right, there was no room for impartiality. Similar problems might be expected to attend the differences between liberal and Marxist historians or between theologians who believe that theology must be purely 'confessional' and those who do not.

As I have been using the word 'objective' (following Broady) it is clear, I think, that sociology might in certain respects not be 'objective' while yet admitting of reasonable judgements and so of partiality and impartiality. Sociology, however practised, does involve more than 'operations of a fairly technical kind by which we can come to a decision'. If it is true of the natural scientist, it is true *a fortiori* of the social scientist, that certain important choices depend upon personal judgement. So when these two schools of sociology disagree about the extent to which sociology is objective, the word must have another sense. One thing that the parties disagree about, according to Maurice Broady, is whether sociology can be value-free, and this could be what is meant in this context by 'objective'. But I suspect that the dispute goes deeper than this, and that the parties would think it at least made sense to ask the question 'Are values objective?' It must, surely, be open to Broady and his like-minded colleagues to argue that sociology both involves value judgements and is objective. So we must ask what sense of 'objective' would make this possible.

The required sense is, I suggest, something like this: a question is objective if it is the case that, where two people disagree about the answer, at least one of them must be mistaken. Those who assume that, if sociology involves value judgements, it cannot be objective, are just assuming that value judgements are not objective in this sense.

Now there is a very strong tendency among academics to circumscribe rather narrowly the area in which objectivity in this sense is possible. Even if this area is not confined to 'the rigorous core' of a subject, in relation to which a more or less agreed decision-procedure exists, it is often thought not to extend to questions of value or to questions of world-view. Sharing this tendency, academics then divide into two camps. One maintains that these wider questions are not suitable for academic study and that universities can and should eschew them. The other contends that if universities ignore them, they are failing in their duty to their students and to society; and that, in any case, it is only by unashamedly begging questions that they *can* ignore them. But, since it is assumed by both parties that these questions are not 'objective' in the new sense we have given that word, those who think it proper to discuss them are led to feel that in so doing they must sacrifice the ideal of academic impartiality. Then the way is open to ideological propaganda of the most blatant kind.

I agree wholeheartedly with Maurice Broady in his approach to this alleged dilemma. He argues, if I understand him aright, that sociologists and other academics are not called upon to be neutral about values, but are called upon to be impartial; that means to listen to what their opponents have to say and to weigh their evidence and assess their arguments fairly and sympathetically. They are not morally free to cast slurs upon the integrity of those who disagree with them, or to use other rhetorical devices to prevent their case being properly heard, or to manipulate the processes of academic government in order to deny them employment or promotion.

It seems to me to follow that even in relation to these larger, ideological, debates there is in principle the possibility of rational decision. One can seriously attempt to weigh evidence and assess arguments employed by one's opponents only if one admits that they may have genuine force against one's own position. A theoretical system of any kind (and world-views are, at least, theoretical systems, though more than that) develops precisely by coming to terms with counter-examples and counter-arguments, by which it is threatened and may in the end be defeated. The reason why argument on more fundamental questions of moral, political and religious standpoint is so often ineffective is not that argument is here inappropriate, but that the questions are enormously complex and extensively ramified, so that there are many different ways of dealing with refractory evidence. Characteristically the central postulates of the system are protected from alteration as long as possible and modifications are made at the periphery; and the impression is thus created that no counter-arguments will ever be allowed to count against the fundamental assertions of the system. This tendency is not unreasonable, for unless some 'principle of tenacity' is accepted, the system will not be persevered with long enough for its potentialities to be thoroughly explored and tested. And where a man's whole philosophy of life is in question there are good practical reasons why he should not readily give it up (as well as obvious psychological explanations why he does not). Nevertheless, even fundamental principles may have to be abandoned or modified if the entire system that is based upon them becomes steadily less capable than its rivals of accommodating fresh observations and experience.

If, however, he and I are right in holding that impartiality implies that the issues in relation to which one has a duty to be impartial are such that, if two people disagree about them, at least one of them must be mistaken, we are committed to rejecting the relativism of some of Maurice Broady's sociological colleagues. And this in itself raises some difficult ethical problems.

We hold that, as academics, we ought to be fair to those who differ from us; but this means being fair to those who accept this relativist position. So far there is no problem. We shall exert ourselves to be fair to them, that is to say we shall listen carefully to what they say and shall give due weight to the arguments they advance, discounting only what is mere ideological propaganda unsupported, or inadequately supported, by argument. So long as, but only so long as, they themselves observe this academic ethic of impartiality in relation to their opponents, we shall allow them freely to teach and examine. But, they may complain, this is not enough. For we are saying in effect that we permit them academic freedom only on condition that they accept our ethical principles and, in so far as these presuppose certain 'metaphysical' positions, in so far as they accept them too. But this is not being fair to them, for it permits them freedom on our terms, not on theirs.

Let us consider an example of what this means in practice. Let us imagine a university teacher who is committed to a particular ideology, and it is part of this ideology to maintain that only those who start from certain presuppositions and reach certain conclusions are to be allowed freedom of expression. He therefore instils these presuppositions into his students, so far as he is able, and, in his capacity as an examiner, grades candidates according to their orthodoxy and not according to the skill and fairness with which they present their views, whatever they may happen to be. Should he be allowed to examine? And can he reasonably complain if he is not? I suggest that the answer to both questions is 'No'. For, if he appeals to the notion of academic freedom which I have been expounding, that concept allows freedom only on conditions, one of which is that those who enjoy such freedom observe impartiality. If, on the other hand, he appeals to his own ideology, he can scarcely object if we stand pat on ours. Unless, that is, he is prepared to provide us with a rational case for our changing our allegiance. But any such appeal carries with it an implicit acceptance of the ethic of impartiality.

He can, of course, consistently, regard the entire academic arena as the setting for a power struggle in which each side endeavours by non-violent or violent persuasion to capture the control of the university (or the department). In such a struggle he may be prepared to work through the constitutional machinery of the university and to make use of 'arguments', although he does not regard himself as constrained by either. In that case he cannot reasonably complain if the university takes steps to protect itself against him, though he can and will actually complain.

What emerges clearly from this example is that the liberal university is committed to certain values and cannot survive their rejection.

The liberal university need not claim that the social sciences, or other academic disciplines, are value-free, nor need it deny that there are matters of importance about which the truth is in essentials known; but it must insist that, if values are involved, they are open to rational discussion, and that even known or generally accepted truths are open to criticism. There is room, therefore, for a university to be formally associated with a particular world-view, so long as that world-view allows free critical discussion. It can properly, for example, be a place of 'religion' so long as it is also genuinely a place of 'education and learning'.

If my argument is correct, there is a variety of liberalism which is not sufficient of itself to generate an academic ethic, and may indeed threaten it. This is the variety which bases freedom of thought and expression not, like John Milton and J. S. Mill, on the need to discover truth, but simply and solely on the individual's right to self-expression. Creativity, unconstrained by concern for truth, is a powerful disruptive force, and it may be that the weakness of some liberal academics in their resistance to disruption has derived from the essentially Romantic character of their liberal ideals. If what matters is simply that views genuinely held be freely expressed, and if the question of their truth is not considered, or is believed not to arise, it is natural to value them for the sincerity and intensity with which they are held; and that is a criterion that generally favours fanaticism. This romantic tradition has an important contribution to make to our concept of the liberal university so long as it is limited and controlled by a countervailing emphasis on reason.

The liberal university is, or approximates to, what John Lucas calls 'the Areopagite Society'. This is a society in which men have 'a common propensity to prefer the true to the false, the rational to the irrational, *when the issue is put to them*'[4] and in which it is recognised that truth is not easily achieved nor the methods of achieving it entirely non-controversial. 'The Areopagite arguments hold only because truth is both many-sided and shareable by all, if not by all shared; only because different people reason differently, but yet all can hope to agree on the validity of reasons adduced.'[5]

It is obviously not possible for an entire nation state to approximate as closely as a university can do to this Areopagite ideal, and it is an essential function of a university in a broadly liberal society to give institutional expression to this idea. It is not the least important purpose of a university education to cultivate the habit of impartiality in its students as well as that of objectivity. Any defence of the university against its critics which neglects this consideration is seriously inadequate. It follows that the university ought not to be prepared to undertake a social role, however desirable in itself, which is incompatible with this requirement.

8

NEUTRALITY AND COMMITMENT*

There was a period in last Michaelmas Term during which Ian Ramsey was discharging concurrently the duties of the Bishop of Durham and of the Nolloth Professor. No one who knows him can doubt that he could have continued to do so indefinitely and, in my present position, I cannot help wishing that our arrangements in this University had been flexible enough to permit such pluralism. As it is, he has departed, leaving a gap which no one else could fill. Fortunately he will continue to make his own unique contribution to the philosophy of religion, and it would be premature as well as presumptuous for me to attempt now to assess that contribution. It is perhaps enough to say that during his sixteen years in this chair, if I may so put it, much ice was broken and many bells were set ringing.

There are two things one may try to do in an Inaugural Lecture. One may try to provide an example or specimen of the type of intellectual activity appropriate to the discipline one represents; or one may endeavour to place that discipline in its context and to vindicate it against its critics, if it has any. Ian Ramsey in his lecture on 'Miracles: An Essay in Logical Mapwork'[1] chose the first course. I propose to take the second – although when the discipline is philosophy the distinction is not clear-cut. An attempt to vindicate the philosophy of the Christian religion as an academic

* Originally read as the Inaugural Lecture as Nolloth Professor of the Philosophy of the Christian Religion, Oxford University, 13 May 1968. Published as *Neutrality and Commitment* (Oxford: Oxford University Press, 1968).

subject will be to some extent – or at any rate should be – a philosophical exercise.

It is called for because there are some philosophers and also some theologians who are uneasy about the whole notion of 'the philosophy of the Christian religion'; who would regard it as at the worst a scandal, at the best an anomaly in the intellectual scene. It is not easy to locate precisely the basis of these suspicions – partly because the conventions of polite intercourse in an academic society tend to restrain people from explaining to the holder of a chair just in what ways and to what degree his subject falls short of intellectual respectability. It may be – indeed I hope it is – that these suspicions are felt less strongly and less widely than I suppose; but I am inclined to feel some of them myself, and for that reason alone I welcome an opportunity to examine them.

To begin with there is a double complaint: that the subject is both too small and too large; too small as being confined to the philosophical study of a single religion; too large in that its scope has to be as wide as that of Christianity itself, which, in its cognitive aspect, attempts to lay hold of supernatural mysteries and relate them to all the objects of our theoretical or practical concern. It looks as if the philosophy of religion is committed to large-scale operations of the sort which the academic mind instinctively distrusts. It is not just that the possibility of metaphysics is still to some extent in dispute, but that the concepts with which the philosopher of religion is characteristically concerned include many which, perplexing enough in their more or less everyday employment, are even more problematic and refractory in a theological context. The concepts of existence, necessity, causality, identity, of time and space, of freedom, of explanation (to name only a few) are in any case so difficult that it could quite reasonably be argued that a respectable philosopher would confine himself to prolegomena, and not venture to discuss their religious application.

A further objection would be somewhat less charitable than these. It would be, quite simply, that the project is not only difficult, but known in advance to be unrewarding. As one philosopher put it to me, with exemplary candour and conciseness: 'Christianity is a set of false stories of no intrinsic interest.' And if this is so, the available philosophical resources could be applied more economically to other topics.

Finally, there is, I suspect, an uneasy, largely unformulated suspicion that the subject is one which cannot in practice, and perhaps cannot even in principle, be treated with the neutrality proper to philosophy; a suspicion not entirely allayed by the abolition, in the case of this chair, of the religious test. And matching this suspicion there is another on the part of some theologians that such neutrality, if attainable, would be incompatible with the commitment which Christian faith demands.

This last question, which in one form or another agitates both philosophers and theologians, is, as my title indicates, the one which I chiefly want to discuss. But before I do so, I think it would be useful to comment briefly on the others.

The complaint that the subject is too small amounts, in fact, to two complaints. One of them is comparatively trivial and easily disposed of. The philosophy of the Christian religion may appear to be a narrowly confined subject, but it would be hard to find a philosophical issue of importance which is not raised in it. Philosophy is, in a sense, indivisible; and the common subdivisions, philosophical logic, philosophy of mind, moral and political philosophy, philosophy of science, *etc.*, represent differences of subject-matter but involve the same analytical methods and similar patterns of argument.

But the complaint may be directed more specifically against the limitation to the *Christian* religion. Would it not make for a more balanced and impartial treatment if all religions, or religion as such, were the object of philosophical investigation? In part the answer to this must be a pragmatic one. We need to know what we are talking about, and in our faculties of theology there are readily available for the study of the Judaeo-Christian tradition the very considerable linguistic, historical, and exegetical resources which are needed to make sure we do. Moreover, students are here moving in a world of thought which is familiar. The Christian religion has inspired and continues to inspire much of our culture, and it is the religion which most of us have been brought up in, have rebelled against, been reconciled to, or continue to be troubled by.

But there are more theoretical reasons. There is, after all, no such religion as 'religion as such', and the attempt to formulate a definition of religion which will fit all religions (even if we confine ourselves to the 'higher religions') is likely to result in something so vague that one cannot get any kind of intellectual grip on it, and something, moreover, which the serious adherent of any particular religion cannot recognise as that to which he is committed, nor its serious opponent as that to which he objects. This is not to say that the comparative study of religion is not possible from a philosophical point of view; only that it has to be genuinely comparative. The student must familiarise himself with the language and the literature, the history and the contemporary practice of each of the religions, and must then actually compare them without assuming from the start that they have certain fundamental concepts and concerns in common, though he may well discover in the end that they have. This is the sort of study of religion which is undertaken by such scholars as Professor Zaehner and Professor Smart, and the mention of their names is enough to show its value for the philosophy of religion. But it involves and cannot replace the philosophical examination of the Christian religion as an activity in its own right. Moreover, to understand another religion involves an effort of imaginative sympathy which is unlikely to be successful, unless it is based on close familiarity with some particular religious tradition.

The objection on the score of *smallness* does not, then, worry me much. The objection on the score of *largeness* is much more formidable. It does seem dangerously presumptuous to embark upon the discussion of concepts as difficult as those necessarily involved in the examination of religious belief. The academic's suspicion of large-scale intellectual enterprises is not without justification. The plain man's temptation is always to generalise too readily, to believe uncritically whatever he wants to believe, and our academic inhibitions are a valuable safeguard against these tendencies. In the field of religion they may well seem to be especially needed. Nevertheless this justifiable caution can itself constitute a temptation, which ought to be resisted, to eschew discussion of important issues for no better reason than that they are important; and then to regard as important the lesser issues one has chosen to discuss. In this matter I believe that academics have a duty to help maintain the level of public debate. People will in fact discuss the questions they believe to be important, no matter how difficult, delicate, or controversial they may be, or how problematic the concepts they involve. In the present state of lively controversy about religion in relation to such matters as education and personal and social ethics, those of us who live and work in universities must make what contribution we can to the elucidation of the issues.

There is also, I suggest, a more technical reason why it would be a mistake to postpone indefinitely the consideration of specifically religious uses of language. Granted that it is a controversial question whether for instance there is a proper use of the expression 'necessary being' as employed in traditional philosophical theology, it is a question which could only be answered after a thorough examination of the role which it performs, or is believed to perform, in its full theological context. The same might be said about the concept of causality as applied to divine activity. It is tempting, therefore, to say, 'Let us work patiently on the concepts of necessity, existence and causality as they are found in less controversial settings, and then, when we have sorted them out, let us see how, if at all, they work in religious discourse.' But what is all too likely to happen, if this policy is exclusively adopted, is that an analysis which fits a certain range of non-religious uses will be taken to exhaust the concepts of necessity, existence, or causality, as the case may be, and the alleged religious uses will be dismissed as illegitimate without ever having been treated as serious candidates for consideration. And this may well be unsatisfactory, not only because it begs the religious question, but because it encourages philosophers to over-simplify. For it is possible that if the religious cases were taken seriously, they might illuminate some features of their more everyday uses which the initial analysis had overlooked or distorted.

That Christianity comprises a set of false stories of no intrinsic interest is, if the premiss be accepted, a sufficient reason for not wasting philosophical manpower on it. My presence here is, perhaps, a clear enough indication that I do not accept the premiss. I do not intend, for obvious reasons, to discuss that question now. But it is perhaps worth reminding ourselves, simply as a matter of historical fact, that there is scarcely a historical philosopher of consequence who has not interested himself in philosophical theology. It may be true, as Mr Strawson has recently remarked, that 'it is with very moderate enthusiasm that a twentieth-century philosopher approaches the subject of philosophical theology',[2] but it is not true of his predecessors. Plato, Aristotle, Aquinas, Descartes, Locke, Berkeley, Hume, Spinoza, Leibniz, Kant, Hegel – to name only the most familiar. If we easily forget this, it is because of the extremely selective way in which we tend to treat the history of philosophy, looking in it for what will illustrate and illuminate our contemporary interests. Educationally there is obviously a good deal to be said for this, but there is no denying that the results can give a very lop-sided impression of the history of ideas. I am ashamed to say that I only recently became acquainted with the syllabus for the philosophy of religion paper in the Theology School. Undergraduates are invited to read, among other things, Locke's *On the Reasonableness of Christianity*, Butler's *Analogy*, and Hume's *Dialogues concerning Natural Religion* – all works as interesting philosophically as they are illustrative of the intellectual concerns of their authors. It is instructive to compare this with the average Greats man's view of God; seen first in *The Republic* creating the Form of Bed (although it is clear from the *Timaeus* that Plato believed that God did not create the Forms); then in Descartes, where he is invoked to dispel the malignant demon whom Descartes has gratuitously invented to justify his scepticism about logic and mathematics. He is absent in Locke, who tends to be seen through the eyes of Berkeley as if he were an atheist. In Berkeley himself he appears chiefly as a fifth wheel on the coach of phenomenalism. He probably receives no further mention until in *Language, Truth and Logic* a hypothesis which has long been superfluous is now finally declared to be also unintelligible. That this picture is very little exaggerated I am well placed to know, because for twenty years I have regularly assisted in painting it. It is perhaps as well that somewhere in our syllabuses the balance should be redressed.

I come now to the problem which provides the title for my lecture, and which I think gives rise to the most serious of the worries some people have about the philosophy of the Christian religion as an academic subject. Crudely put, the problem is this. Philosophers suspect that the philosopher of religion cannot achieve proper philosophical neutrality. Theologians suspect that he cannot maintain necessary Christian commitment.

In this form the difficulty arises only when the philosopher of religion is himself a believer. As such, it would seem, he is committed to certain beliefs which, in his religious life and thought, are not put in issue. But, as a philosopher, he cannot be so committed, for a philosopher proceeds, as Plato puts it, 'by destroying assumptions'. It is hard, then, to see how a man can genuinely be a philosopher, if some questions are not open for him. Moreover (it might be thought), the sort of man who can at all commit himself as the Christian must, lacks the intellectual honesty which the practice of philosophy demands. Some such feelings as these may lie behind the attitude of those who would be rather happier if the Nolloth Professor were an atheist, and even, perhaps, of some of those who are glad that he is a layman and, therefore, not quite so committed as he would have to be if he were a clergyman.

There is, I think, a genuine problem here – and probably more than one. It is worth noticing, to begin with, that to a very considerable extent this problem is a special case of one which confronts any academic who has to reconcile the demands of scholarly caution and detachment with the need to develop and maintain a consistent 'philosophy of life'. If the tension is more acute for philosophers than for most, it is because philosophy touches life, at least potentially, at all points.

Descartes recognises the problem and formulates his own answer to it in Part III of the *Discourse*:

> And finally, as it is not enough before commencing to rebuild the house in which we live, that it be pulled down and builders provided, or that we engage in the work ourselves, according to a plan which we have beforehand carefully drawn out, but as it is likewise necessary that we be furnished with some other house in which we may live commodiously during the operations, so that I might not remain irresolute in my actions, while my reason compelled me to suspend my judgement, and that I might not be prevented from living thenceforward in the greatest possible felicity, I formed a provisory code of morals, composed of three or four maxims . . .[3]

The first was 'to obey the laws and customs of my country, adhering firmly to the faith in which, by the grace of God, I had been educated from my childhood . . .'[4]

The second was 'to be as firm and resolute in my actions as I was able, and not to adhere less steadfastly to the most doubtful opinions, when once adopted, than if they had been highly certain'.[5]

Descartes, of course, sees it as only a temporary predicament, for he is going within measurable time to build all things new on the foundations uncovered by methodical doubt. So his solution is only an *interims-ethik*. And he oversimplifies. Philosophical enquiry does not exhaust the whole of what one means by 'reason' and, presumably, Descartes would choose to adhere to those 'doubtful opinions' which were, in some sense, more reasonable than others. Nevertheless I think he appreciates the basic dilemma. A man cannot remain perpetually irresolute about the principles on which he is to live his life. At some point he must decide where he stands and, having decided, should not allow himself to be 'carried about with every wind of doctrine'. And this for the sort of reason that Burke advances when he recommends adherence to prejudice 'with the reason involved', rather than relying simply on 'the naked reason':

> because prejudice with its reason, has a motive to give action to that reason, and an affection that will give it permanence. Prejudice is of ready application in the emergency; it previously engages the mind in a steady course of wisdom and virtue, and does not leave the man hesitating in the moment of decision, sceptical, puzzled, and unresolved. Prejudice renders a man's virtue his habit; and not a series of unconnected acts. Through just prejudice, his duty becomes a part of his nature.[6]

This does not mean that such fundamental decisions are incapable of being rationally defended (Burke himself talks of 'prejudice with the reason involved'); still less does it mean that there could never be sufficient reason for changing one's mind; but it does mean that one should maintain a steady course and not fluctuate continually.

I am not advocating a kind of obscurantism (which Burke, to be sure, sometimes gets close to doing). I would suggest, rather, that some such policy as Descartes adopted is a necessary condition both of practical effectiveness and of philosophical independence. A man who is prepared to accept in everyday life for true nothing which he cannot philosophically defend will either become practically ineffective and humanly incomplete, or else philosophically unadventurous. From this point of view the tendency of philosophers to pursue speculations in their studies, which they proceed to ignore as soon as they are out of them, may not be simply an index of the moral weakness of the profession, but a necessary corollary of philosophical activity.

If there is any truth in what I have been saying, it will, of course, apply to religion as well as to any consistent view of life. Bertrand Russell recounts somewhere how one morning as a young man he was walking in Cambridge and there suddenly burst upon him the thought 'Great God in boots – the ontological argument is sound!'[7] If a similar experience were tomorrow to befall Professor Ayer, he would not, I am suggesting, be manifesting intellectual dishonesty if he did not at once abandon his deeply felt and long-matured views upon religious belief. In the end, indeed, he might do so, but it would have to be the culmination of a process in which much more was involved than purely philosophical enquiry.

Why is this? There are two features in particular of the complex pattern of beliefs and attitudes which constitute the individual's philosophy of life which make it rightly slow to respond to philosophical (or other 'rational') criticism. The first is that it is and can be only partly articulate. Indeed it is this feature which makes philosophical analysis both necessary and difficult. If a man, even a highly educated and literate man, is asked to write an article on 'What I believe', what he succeeds in enunciating is only an incomplete and misleadingly simple account of the considerations which in fact guide his thinking and acting. He is painfully aware that he cannot put these adequately into words. The second is that, even if he does not consciously identify himself with some particular tradition as the religious believer does, he has in fact been influenced by innumerable currents of thought which affect the language he uses and reflect as yet unidentified assumptions and arguments. This is, I take it, what Burke means by 'prejudice with the reason involved'. Because the reason *is* 'involved' and able to be disentangled only with care and patience, the business of assessing it is far more laborious and uncertain than at first it seems – and certainly far more than Descartes thought it was. It is less like building a new house than gradually restoring and converting the house in which one lives, knowing that the operations will last for many generations.

In such a situation the individual cannot help being aware of his own limitations, as he constantly finds himself sensing, or thinking that he senses, that something is wrong with this piece of argument, or promising in that, without being acute enough to identify it there and then.

If, because of these characteristics of a 'philosophy of life', it is unreasonable to allow it to be too readily responsive to philosophical criticism, there are also certain features of academic work (in philosophy, as in other disciplines) which tend to justify this caution. For what I have said about a 'philosophy of life' is also true to a lesser extent of the actual practice of professional philosophers. Although philosophy, abstractly conceived, may be entirely 'open' in the way Plato so splendidly declares, its practice at any particular time and place and by individual persons is inevitably guided by assumptions which are questionable, but not there and then questioned or even recognised. Indeed it is hard to see how any subject could progress without the immediate focus of intense and concentrated interest being determined by a tacit agreement to leave certain other questions untouched. This is perhaps why all academic disciplines, outside the exact sciences, are so susceptible to fashions and so sensitive to the *Zeitgeist*. This characteristic of academic work is as a rule most easily noticeable in the practice of one's colleagues in other subjects. No one, for example, who is not himself a literary critic or a sociologist or an economist can fail to discern in them a tendency to repudiate today what they were vigorously maintaining yesterday; and if I school myself to look with an impartial eye I fancy that I notice a similar tendency even in philosophers.

Indeed, an analogous problem breaks out within each academic discipline itself. There is a constant tension between commitment and openness in the day-to-day work of philosophers, scientists, historians, and others. In none of these fields does one abandon a promising hypothesis as soon as it encounters difficulties, even difficulties which seem for the time being insuperable. One reformulates the hypothesis, one admits gaps in the argument, one hazards the guess that it will in the end turn out in such and such a way, one backs one's hunch.

It seems to me, then, that any philosopher (and *mutatis*

mutandis, any academic) has this problem of reconciling his neutrality as a philosopher with his commitment as a man, and that it exposes him to a double temptation, that of distorting the philosophical arguments so as to bring them into line with his personal commitment, and that of abandoning his personal commitment prematurely when the philosophical going gets difficult.

To put it in this way implies, what I believe to be the case, that one cannot rule out the possibility that what has hitherto presented itself as a temptation to be resisted should in the end come to be seen as a legitimate demand that one alter or abandon one's position. There is a celebrated passage in Hume which reflects this predicament:

> Very refined speculations have little or no influence upon us; and yet we do not and cannot establish it for a rule, that they ought not to have any influence; which implies a manifest contradiction. But what have I said, that reflections very refined and metaphysical have little or no influence upon us? This opinion I can scarce forbear retracting and condemning from my present feeling and experience. The intense view of these manifold contradictions and imperfections in human reason has so wrought upon me, and heated my brain, that I am ready to reject all belief and reasoning and can look upon no opinion even as more probable or likely than another. Where am I, or what? From what causes do I derive my existence and to what condition shall I return? Whose favour shall I court, and whose anger must I dread? What beings surround me? And on whom have I any influence, or who have any influence on me? I am confounded with all these questions and begin to fancy myself in the most deplorable condition imaginable, environed with the deepest darkness, and utterly deprived of the use of every member and faculty.
>
> Most fortunately it happens that since reason is incapable of dispelling these clouds, nature herself suffices to that purpose, and cures me of this philosophical melancholy and delirium, either by relaxing the bent of my mind, or by some avocation and lively impression of my senses which

obliterates all these chimeras. I dine, I play a game of backgammon, I converse and am merry with my friends; and when, after three or four hours' amusement, I would return to these speculations, they appear so cold, so strained and ridiculous that I cannot find it in my heart to enter into them any further.[8]

And so Hume concludes (in a manner reminiscent of Descartes): 'Here then I find myself absolutely and necessarily determined to live and talk and act like other people in the common affairs of life . . .'[9]

Hume's irony cannot conceal from us the fact that he has not resolved the problems which he has so clearly stated: 'Very refined speculations have little or no influence upon us; *and yet we do not and cannot establish it for a rule, that they ought not to have any influence.*'[10] I should not wish to underestimate the benevolent effects of backgammon or its modern equivalents, or of the remedy which Hume elsewhere recommends, 'carelessness and inattention', but on Hume's own admission the problem is a moral and not just a psychological one.

So far I have been treating the question of Christian commitment and philosophical neutrality as a special case of a more general problem, but it would be idle to deny that the problem is more acute for the religious believer, for he is committed not only to the acceptance of certain propositions, but to faith in God and loyalty to the Church as an institution. And this means that his commitment to certain beliefs, since it is bound up with something analogous to faith in a person, is of a different order from the commitment any man may have to a philosophy of life, which he is free at any time to abandon without incurring a charge of disloyalty. I have tried elsewhere to consider precisely in what the difference consists. It complicates the present problem, without, I think, altering it in essentials. The problem in its specifically religious form is familiar to us in the traditional debate about faith and reason. And, in terms of that debate, what I have been maintaining is that there is and ought to be a tension between faith and reason.

However, it may be objected that in presenting the problem in the way I have done, I have totally misconceived the character both of philosophy and of theology, and that, given a proper understanding of the role of philosophy and religion, a conflict of the sort I have tried to analyse cannot conceivably occur. Broadly speaking, the argument would be either (or both) that philosophy is innocuous or that religion is invulnerable. The most tempting way of seeking to show that religion is invulnerable to attack on philosophical, scientific, or historical grounds is to deny that religion makes any factual claims, an approach which has been much canvassed from Kant to the present day. If this is so, then my dilemma fails of application because the religious believer, although committed, is not committed to the acceptance of any propositions, and so cannot be disturbed by doubts about their truth or their significance. I do not now intend to discuss this view of religious belief, which seems to me in the end to avoid risk at the cost of sterility.

Instead I shall start from the philosophical end and the claim that philosophy is neutral in such a way as to make it powerless to exercise any influence upon the question of the validity of religious belief. Philosophy, it would be said by supporters of this position, is not 'reason' in the sense required by the old antithesis and can have no tendency either to support or to weaken faith. According to this view philosophy is neutral not only in the sense I have hitherto employed of 'not committed to any prior assumptions' but also in the sense of 'not adjudicating upon matters of fact'. Philosophy is concerned with the analysis of concepts and the assessment of arguments; it has nothing to say about the way things are. The philosophy of science does not seek to establish or refute scientific hypotheses, nor the philosophy of history to dictate the methods of historical research. Political philosophy does not presume to tell us how we should be governed, or moral philosophy how we should live. Similarly the philosophy of religion can have nothing to say about particular religious beliefs.

Nothing could be more reassuring than such a modest

declaration of philosophical neutrality or more devastating than the operations it nevertheless permits. For it is necessarily asymmetrical. Philosophy cannot give any support to a religious position, but it can stigmatise religious concepts as self-contradictory or in other ways logically incoherent and, in the hands of some of its practitioners, has often done so. The neutrality of philosophy, so understood, is not the neutrality of a non-belligerent neighbour, but rather that of an international peace-keeping force which has strict instructions to assist neither side in a conflict, but can annihilate one of them if it chooses without any violation of neutrality. Yet, if the philosopher is to examine characteristically religious concepts and arguments, he must, it would seem, be free to conclude in the light of his examination that some or all of them are radically unsatisfactory, or in need of extensive revision.

Against this it has been urged by thinkers under the influence of Wittgenstein, reinforcing a fideist strand in theology itself, that religious faith can only be judged by criteria intrinsic to religion. 'This language-game is played'; the associated form of life goes on. It does not make sense to say that it stands in need of justification or is open to correction or refutation, any more than, it is argued, it would make sense to say such things about history, law, or morality. 'Philosophy leaves everything as it is.' On this view the job of the peace-keeping force is to identify and patrol the frontiers between the various parties; it sees that they do not encroach upon one another, and has no power to encroach itself.

This account might have some plausibility if certain conditions were satisfied, (1) if the frontiers were capable of being clearly defined, (2) if there were no disputes about the frontiers, and (3) if no claims were made to exercise influence or authority beyond the frontiers. In the case of religion it seems clear that these conditions do not hold. Christianity, for example, involves certain assertions about the past which are part of its creed, although in a perfectly straightforward sense historical, *i.e.* belonging to the subject-matter of academic history and open to study by its methods – 'crucified under Pontius Pilate'. Other assertions like those concerning the resurrection also refer ostensibly to events in the past, although it is a controversial question whether or to what extent they are open to ordinary historical investigation. Partly this is because there are differences of opinion between theologians as to the proper interpretation of the resurrection; partly because the boundaries of history are not beyond dispute. A historian's judgement as to what *did* happen is inevitably affected by his conception of what *could* happen, and this may be influenced by his entire world-view.

Similar questions arise about the relationship between religion and science in connection with, say, the miraculous. It is, of course, legitimate to argue that, given a proper understanding of the claims of religion, no conflict with science or history need occur. But it is hard to see how one could guarantee this result, in advance of careful investigation, except by taking care so to interpret the religious claims that no collision with empirically discovered fact is even in principle conceivable. And then the question is whether Christianity, so interpreted, can any longer have the relevance to human life and the authority over it which it has traditionally claimed, and whether it can still make sense of those features of our experience which most insistently demand a religious response.

The position is further complicated by the fact that religion untarnished by theology is a romantic dream, and theology must to a great extent concern itself with issues which are recognisably philosophical. Theology is like any other academic subject in not being a single homogeneous system. It is rather an area of lively controversy, within which philosophical conceptions of diverse ancestry are frequently invoked. It really is asking too much of a philosophical frontier patrol to refrain altogether from taking a hand in these internal disputes, especially when the theologians so often seem to treat their philosophical mercenaries with quite exaggerated respect.

It has, of course, been seriously argued that religion is, in virtue of its subject-matter, a special case, possessing an invulnerability to philosophical criticism which is not shared by other types of human culture. I cannot now examine these arguments. My own impression is that the philosophy of religion is not differently placed from the 'philosophy of' anything else. The philosopher of history discusses such questions as these: What is the character of historical explanation? How, if at all, does it differ from explanation in the natural sciences? Does history offer explanations at all? In what sense, if at all, is history as a discipline objective? What are the criteria for the correctness of historical judgements? The philosophy of law examines such problems as the nature of criminal responsibility and the justification of the legal system. In both cases a proposal to decide these questions by 'criteria intrinsic to the discipline itself' would run into difficulties, unless taken simply as a salutary warning against the neat and uncritical application of criteria drawn from elsewhere. There is in both cases an overlap with psychology and sociology, with a possible threat of a complete takeover; and in neither case can judgements of value be totally excluded.

To take a specific example. It would surely be rash to assume in advance that historical explanation either conforms to the pattern of explanation in the physical sciences or is not properly to be regarded as explanation at all. Yet neither will it do simply to accept without examination the claim of most (but not all) historians to be offering explanations of a different type. A very careful and sympathetic examination of what the historian actually does is required. But who *is* 'the historian'? There are significant differences between historians in their methods and sometimes about their methods. This is nicely illustrated in a recent review in the *Observer* in which Mr A. J. P. Taylor writes: 'The explanations are clear and often convincing. They certainly make the past more comprehensible than my own view, which is simply: "Things happen because they happen." Of course it is possible that my explanation is the truer.' It is hard to see how the philosopher of history can avoid taking sides in these internal disputes. But who *is* 'the philosopher'? Here too there are notorious differences of method and of presuppositions.

If there is anything in what I have been saying, the sort of frontier patrol that is needed is much more like a boundaries commission which is not committed in advance to maintaining the *status quo*, but endeavours impartially to judge the claims put to it and to draw lines and apportion spheres of influence where it is overall best for them to be. It would not be neutral in the sense that its activities made no difference to the final pattern; it would be neutral in the sense that it listened only to arguments and tried to judge them fairly; which is no more than to say that it engaged in a rational activity.

Thus it will not do to maintain *either* that the religious believer's account of his faith is sacrosanct and that no philosophical critique can touch it by way of analysing its concepts or assessing its arguments, *or* that it is open to philosophers to go through religious claims and check their adequacy without making a serious and sympathetic attempt to consider the arguments by which they are supported. A philosopher can, of course, argue that religion is, in the end, an illusion and that the 'facts' to which believers call attention are rightly to be interpreted not in terms of certain specifically religious concepts but rather as aberrations explicable by some psychological or sociological theory. But he cannot take some such theory for granted as if it lay wholly outside the realm of philosophical controversy.

In the light of this discussion about the nature of philosophical neutrality I do not think that the problem of neutrality and commitment, as I originally posed it, is a factitious one. Religious belief is not inherently invulnerable to philosophical criticism, and therefore the individual who is committed to a religious faith incurs a risk of possible refutation, as he does if he adopts any coherent 'philosophy of life'.

As I have conceded, there are arguments, both theological and philosophical, which purport to show that the conflict can be avoided. Descartes thought it was only temporary – until he had once and for all ascertained the truth. Kant's entire philosophy could be represented as a sustained attempt to resolve it at a theoretical level. But I think that Hume was right in seeing it as essentially a practical moral problem. For none of the theories which claim to dispose of it is entirely free from the very doubts and difficulties which give rise to it. We have not got and are not going to have certainty or anything like it. We never cease learning philosophy; we never plumb the depths of our religion.

How the problem is to be solved, how the balance is to be struck is, in the end, for the individual to judge. What matters, I suggest, in an academic community, is that the tension should be both recognised and regulated. To avoid discussion with intellectual rigour of controversial issues about morality, politics, and religion, about which individuals are or ought to be committed, is likely to lead to one or the other of two undesirable consequences: a reluctance to commit oneself at all; or a refusal to think about or allow others critically to discuss the causes to which one is enthusiastically committed. Rather than aim at a neutrality which is, perhaps in theory, and certainly in practice, unattainable, we should register our commitment to conventions of free, fair, and disciplined debate.

9

FAITH AND REASON:
A FALSE ANTITHESIS?*

'I can't believe that,' said Alice.

'Can't you?' the Queen said in a pitying tone. 'Try again: draw a long breath and shut your eyes.'

Alice laughed. 'There's no use trying,' she said. 'One can't believe impossible things.'

'I dare say you haven't had much practice,' said the Queen. 'Why sometimes I've believed as many as six impossible things before breakfast.'

(Lewis Carroll, *Alice Through the Looking-Glass*)

This familiar passage presents a common view of faith, especially religious faith, and no doubt the Rev. Charles Lutwidge Dodgson, when he wrote it, was well aware of its theological applications. We tend to think of faith as involving effort, the effort required to believe things that are inherently difficult to believe; and the paradigm case of such faith is religious faith. So it becomes almost part of the definition of faith that it is contrary to reason. For the reasonable man bases his beliefs upon evidence and the degree of conviction he allows himself is strictly in proportion to the strength of the evidence. It 'rises and falls' with the evidence. It follows that there is an inevitable opposition between religion and reason; and, since the rational enterprise *par excellence* is science, this becomes an opposition between religion and science, not – at least primarily – in the sense that the findings of religion and science are opposed, but that their methods are. Science is a matter of reason; religion is a matter of faith.

* From *Religious Studies* 16 (1980), pp. 131–44.

If this way of thinking is correct, it has important implications for education. Scientific education will involve the cultivation of the scientific temper, that is to say, the readiness to approach experience with an entirely open mind and the habit of reaching a conclusion only when the evidence clearly supports it. Since, *ex hypothesi*, religious faith is not based on, and does not appeal to, reason, the only way it could be communicated would be by some form of non-rational persuasion or 'indoctrination'. Religious education ought, therefore, either to be abandoned or to be undertaken in an entirely 'objective' or 'phenomenological' way. Children should not be taught Judaism or Christianity or any other religion but rather taught about them.

Contemporary theologians and educational theorists generally respond to this position in one of two ways. The first is to assimilate christianity (or any other religion) to the scientific model and to insist that theology should be an entirely 'open-ended' activity. No more than the scientist should the religious believer regard himself as committed to certain beliefs; like the scientist he should rest his convictions upon human experience and be prepared to modify them as and when new evidence requires it. The second is to attempt a counter-attack upon the scientist and to claim that science itself is based upon a kind of faith in that the scientist accepts certain presuppositions about, for example, causality or the uniformity of nature, without which science could not proceed, but which do not require, and cannot be given, any rational justification. So in the end, both science and religion are matters of faith and not reason. And this counter-attack derives some support from the contemporary disenchantment with 'the technocratic society'; for if the entire scientific enterprise represents the effects of a fundamental non-rational decision which modern man took three or so centuries ago, it is open to us now with no sacrifice of integrity to repudiate it in favour of a radically different option.

The question I want to raise is whether the underlying conception of faith and reason as essentially antithetical, a conception common to both parties in the debate, is itself adequate to an understanding of our intellectual life. And I want in the first instance to enquire how far the problem of faith and reason, or something like it, arises in non-religious contexts; and then, and only then, to consider whether there are any peculiar difficulties about the relation between faith and reason in religion.

Let us begin with science itself. The popular picture of science as an entirely open-ended activity, and of the scientist as concerned to test a hypothesis and accept or reject it on the basis of the experimental evidence alone, corresponds to what T. S. Kuhn calls 'normal science'.[1] In the scientist's day-to-day work there is already in existence and taken entirely for granted by him an accepted theoretical structure, and the individual researcher is testing comparatively low-level hypotheses framed in terms of concepts that belong to that structure. Nothing more fundamental than the hypothesis itself hangs upon the experiment, and he is willing to drop that if the experiment is unsuccessful. The experiment would otherwise have no point. The situation, however, is significantly different, and so is the scientist's attitude, if, in the course of his work, he encounters evidence which calls in question the basic theoretical structure itself or some important part of it. It simply is not the case that he is prepared to give up comparatively fundamental laws in the face of recalcitrant observations or, at any rate, to do so without a struggle. Rather than do this he prefers to adopt other devices – to cast doubt on the observations, or to introduce subsidiary hypotheses to explain the discrepancy, or even sometimes to put the observations in cold storage, so to speak, in the hope (or in the faith?) that a suitable explanation conformable to the existing structure will turn up.

Similarly the editor of a scientific journal is by no means entirely open-minded when deciding what to publish; he attaches a good deal of weight to the authority of established scientists, who act as referees, and he is unlikely to publish something by an unknown researcher which runs strongly counter to the prevailing orthodoxy. To give a specific example, the late Professor Michael Polanyi in his book *Knowing and Being*[2] describes the vicissitudes of his 'potential theory of adsorption'. He advanced this theory early in his career and was quite unable to get a hearing for it. Although it had good experimental backing, it was out of line with the current direction of that branch of chemistry. Some fifty years later it became generally accepted. Polanyi acknowledges the dangers to which science may be exposed through the suppression of promising new ideas, but then gives it as his considered judgement that the leading scientists of the time were right to dismiss his theory. To have taken it seriously would have involved too great a modification of the accepted structure of chemistry as it was then understood.

Hence scientists need what has been called a 'principle of tenacity' to ensure that they do not generally call in question the fundamental laws of their science as they are currently understood (let alone the entire system). There would, indeed, be no point in their doing so, since there is, *ex hypothesi*, no viable alternative at present in sight, and their ability to go on doing effective scientific work depends upon their trusting the existing framework. Thus the notion that scientific theories 'rise and fall with the evidence' is only partially correct. It is true of a particular scientific hypothesis put forward in the course of research which is being conducted against a background of accepted theory. An expert in the field could no doubt say with reasonable confidence just how it stands at the moment – just how well supported it is. The fundamental scientific law is in a very different case. It is so firmly integrated into the system as a whole that nothing but a large-scale Kuhnian revolution could dislodge it.

This is not to say, however, that it cannot be called in question at all – as the second type of response maintains. We have in our own day seen scientists question such apparently basic beliefs as that the speed of light cannot be exceeded or that two events in different places can happen simultaneously or that something cannot just come into existence. Even a comparatively fundamental belief may in the end have to be revised if the time comes when it, or the system of which it is an essential component, can no longer account adequately, or as adequately as some rival theory, for the data of observation.

There are, then, elements of trust and of respect for authority in science which require us to modify to some extent the simple contrast between the open-ended attitude of the scientist and the committed attitude of the man of religious faith. (It is interesting to note, in passing, that another contrast requires also to be modified, *viz.* that between the common-sense credibility of scientific theories and the incredibility of religious dogma: the scientist also, under the pressure of the demand for simplicity and explanatory power, may find himself 'believing six impossible things before breakfast'.)

Nevertheless, even when due allowance has been made for these modifications, they suggest only a rather remote analogy with religious faith. The 'faith' the scientist exhibits is so obvious a requirement of an effective scientific policy that no one would even be tempted to regard faith and reason as antithetical.

The sciences that I have been discussing so far are the natural sciences, which are comparatively unified and whose practitioners very largely agree about fundamentals (although I am assured by philosophers of science that this appearance of unity is to some extent deceptive). In the human sciences and even more obviously in the humanities, there is present not as an occasional phenomenon, but as a regular feature of their operation, a good deal of lively controversy. I need only mention the continuing debate about the relative importance of genetic and environmental factors in the social sciences, conducted often with notable acerbity, and the rival claims of, for example, Skinnerian stimulus-response theory and the various schools of post-Freudian psychodynamics in psychology. That this situation obtains in philosophy or economics is so evident that it scarcely requires illustration. Indeed I think one may generalise and say that the existence of rival 'schools of thought' is, outside the natural sciences, a characteristic feature of academic life, and one which deserves more attention than is usually given it.

In what follows I use the term 'academic' to refer to persons who work in the human sciences or the humanities. If I am right about the prevalence of 'schools of thought' in these areas, the normal situation of the academic is such that:

1. He believes in a certain conception of the way his subject should be treated and has certain views as to what concepts, theories and modes of argument are fundamental to it.

2. In terms of these he believes himself to be in possession of a certain 'body of knowledge' upon which he relies in teaching and research and in making recommendations for practical policy, when called upon to do so.

3. He recognises (or should recognise) that his approach to the subject is not universally accepted and that there exist bodies of scientific and scholarly opinion, of a sort that cannot be entirely discounted, which are to a greater or lesser extent critical of his approach. (I say 'should recognise' because no one acquainted with the facts of academic life can fail to be aware that such recognition is sometimes absent. Far from acknowledging that reasonable men could hold views substantially different from their own, and that some actually do, academics all too often regard their opponents as fools or even knaves.)

4. His way of approaching the subject involves certain judgements, not universally shared, as to what is important and as to what are desirable ends to pursue, and these have implications for practical decisions both inside and outside the academic field.

In this typical situation it is evident, I think, that he will need, even more than the natural scientist does, the capacity to persevere in the face of his own doubts and the criticisms of his colleagues. If the subject, as he understands it, is to develop fruitfully, its characteristic theses require to be tested and modified over a reasonable period of time, and this means that he cannot be prepared to abandon the theories and concepts he judges to be central as soon as he is confronted with evidence that calls them in question. He must instead do his best to square them with the new evidence, and, as we have seen, he has a number of devices open to him. In the last resort he can simply take the line that 'something will turn up' to vindicate them, although he cannot as yet tell what. In the total absence of such a reaction to unfavourable evidence no 'body of knowledge' would ever have time to be built up. The growing child would always be killed by premature antisepsis. Hence the good academic needs to be a determined man, able and willing to persevere in projects and policies he believes in in face of difficulties and uncertainties, as the biographies of eminent scholars and scientists amply testify.

So far I have considered the individual academic as if his problems were purely intellectual ones, but it would be unrealistic to overlook the extent to which even the cloistered scholar is subject to temptations of a non-rational or dubiously rational kind, which relate specifically to his professional work. In particular intellectual fashions are a regular feature – perhaps an unavoidable one – of the academic scene, and it calls for strength of mind to stand out for an approach to his subject which is currently unpopular. The more so because, as Plato recognised, it is often the cleverest people who are the most strongly attracted to such fashions, so that the influence they exert is a psychological force to be reckoned with; and it is one which, in the nature of the case, cannot be treated as merely psychological. The academic may need at one and the same time to resist this force in so far as it threatens his intellectual integrity and independence while yet allowing it due weight in so far as he can see it to have a rational basis.

What I have been saying thus far is open to an obvious objection, *viz.* that, although true, it is of merely psychological interest. No one doubts that academics, like other people, are subject to fashions and to prejudices and are exposed to temptations to which they often yield or to which they respond inappropriately. They have their share in human weakness; but it palpably *is* human weakness. It is not in principle difficult – and it is in principle necessary – to distinguish between (1) reasonable policies for the optimum development of a line of enquiry in the long run, and (2) emotional or attitudinal reactions to the individual's personal predicament which, however understandable, have no rational basis and ought, so far as possible, to be avoided. In particular, it will be objected, it is neither necessary nor desirable that the academic should become identified with a particular school of thought in the way that gives rise to these emotional responses. He need not and should not actually believe in his way of viewing the subject, as the putative analogy with religious faith suggests, but rather should remain fundamentally detached from it. He should regard it as offering the best available programme for future investigation, and he should persevere with it for so long, and only for so long, as the state of the evidence makes it reasonable to do so. Any sort of personal commitment or emotional involvement is out of place. In the intellectual life it is at best a harmless indulgence; whereas it is an essential component of religious faith.

By way of reply to this objection it is, I think, legitimate to stress, in the first instance, how rarely this ideal of academic detachment is actually achieved. The way in which academics typically respond to the conditions of academic life is by exhibiting the emotional reactions and the active tendencies which are marks of genuine conviction. I know of one university where the department of social science had to be formally divided on account of an irreconcilable conflict between the proponents of two rival approaches to the subject; and it is my impression that if one is looking for *odium theologicum* in the contemporary academic scene one is more likely to find it among the social scientists than among the theologians who treat one another's pronouncements with an altogether suspicious tolerance. That such reactions are excessive may readily be granted, but the resemblance to the excesses which have sometimes characterised religious faith is close enough to be suggestive. One thing that it suggests is that it may not normally be possible for a man to sustain the rigours of academic life while remaining entirely detached from the fray. And if he cannot or can only with difficulty remain detached ought he to try? May it not, for most temperaments at least, be a condition of success that the individual internalise not only the abstract values of impartiality and concern for truth which I take to be the primary academic virtues, but also the attitudes and assumptions characteristic of some particular approach to his subject?

'Success' as so far understood means success in developing a theoretical system; but, as has already been noticed in passing, many academic subjects have practical implications and are engaged in partly for that reason. Many also have – or are believed to have – ideological presuppositions. To the extent that this is so there is a more or less considerable overlap between the positions a man adopts in his academic work and in what may loosely be called his general 'philosophy of life'. And in so far as the former contributes to and is influenced by the latter, it comes to play a part in his personal and social life that is more than merely theoretical. It affects the sort of man he is and helps form his conception of the sort of man he ought to be. A topical illustration of this relationship might be the economics and the politics of Milton Friedman. There is, as comment in the press has emphasised, a fairly close fit between his economic and his political beliefs of such a kind that it is hard to credit that he is committed to the latter, but treats the former with complete intellectual detachment.

Hence I am inclined to suggest that the academic normally requires, and characteristically exhibits, a kind of faith; and moreover that it is reasonable for him to do so. That is to say he adheres to, and believes in, certain schemes of thought of which the following can be said:

1. They are based on evidence and have a rational structure.

2. They are open to criticism and are, as a rule, in fact criticised by those who adopt rival positions.

3. Although one of them may in fact be better based than its rivals, it is not unchallengeably so.

4. They often involve presuppositions of an ideological kind and may have practical implications.

5. They derive from historical traditions of varying ancestries.

6. They are of such complexity that the individual is, as a rule, expert in only part of them and is, therefore, inevitably dependent upon authority to some extent for his understanding of them. He could not provide a clear and articulate justification of his own for all that he accepts from them.

7. They are such that the individual cannot in practice avoid a decision as to whether he accepts them or not; and, in so far as he accepts them, they help to determine the sort of man he is going to be. His 'faith' consists in his determination to adhere to the scheme of thought and allow it to influence his character and conduct, notwithstanding that:

(a) There are, and he knows that there are, arguments and evidence that the scheme cannot, so far as he can see, currently accommodate.

(b) He cannot personally provide all the credentials of the system on demand.

(c) He recognises, or at least ought to recognise, that the scheme could turn out in the end to be, in important respects, mistaken (though, of course, he believes it will not).

His faith is constantly being tried in that he is regularly confronted with the arguments of opponents and is not always able to dispose of them. He often has to hang on to his belief, knowing all the time that his opponents could be right and himself and his friends wrong.

In claiming that this represents the characteristic predicament of the academic I do not of course wish to claim that all academic work conforms to the pattern I have outlined. Some subjects and some aspects of all subjects are of so narrowly technical a kind that they do not display some of the features in my list, and there are academics who incline to the view that only questions susceptible of such 'objective' treatment are suitable for serious study. I do not now propose to argue against that view, but am content to note that it is not in practice very widely shared.

Nevertheless, even if it be conceded that the academic does require an attitude akin to faith, there remains at least one important respect in which religious faith is unique. Religious faith unites two features which, in so far as they are found in the academic life, are found there separately. Religious faith is essentially 'a faith to live by'. A man looks to his religion for the meaning of his whole existence and not just of selected bits of it, and he expects from it guidance in the entire conduct of his life. It is, or aims to be, both comprehensive and practical. By contrast most academic disciplines are restricted to certain selected aspects or areas of the world. The natural sciences achieve their characteristic clarity and rigour by a deliberate limitation to only certain aspects of what they study, chiefly those capable of quantitative measurement; and even subjects like sociology or history do not in actuality or intention embrace the whole of human life. On the other hand, subjects like metaphysics and theology, which aim at a synoptic vision (and are often suspect on this account), do not have it as their primary function to provide practical guidance. These characteristics of a religious system of belief make it even less manageable than the typical academic discipline – it is even less possible for the individual believer to be reasonably confident that he has mastered all the considerations that are relevant to its truth or falsehood. This need not imply that he can form no reasonable judgement at all – that he can only 'plump' in an entirely non-rational way – but it does mean that any judgement he can make is inevitably far removed from the cool and complete appraisal that an ideally rational being might make if he had all the time in the world and no pressing practical preoccupations. So he is bound to rely to an even larger extent on the authority of others whom he is prepared to trust.

But these characteristics of religious faith are not in themselves uniquely religious. They apply equally to what I earlier called 'philosophies of life', and these, of course, may be entirely secular. In regard to the general conduct of his life a man cannot maintain indefinitely an attitude of academic detachment. He has decisions to make; and the way he makes them will eventually determine the sort of man he becomes. In so far as he endeavours to achieve consistency in his choices and coherence in the reasons he gives for them, he finds himself in fundamentally the same predicament as the man who embraces a religious philosophy of life. The positions he adopts and reasons he relies on will, of course, characteristically be different from those of the religious man, but they will also be to some extent controversial, not only in the sense that they are in fact challenged, but also in the sense that not all the challenges can be discounted as having no rational basis. This is, indeed, the universal human predicament. In everyday life people are constantly required to make decisions in ambiguous situations where, even if they could remain always calm and composed, they would sometimes find it hard to adhere to a consistent policy, but where they are in fact subject to emotional stresses which are liable to affect their imagination and their judgement. They have no choice but to make and stand by decisions in the face of objective uncertainties and subjective temptations. Even if the academic manages to some extent to avoid this predicament in his specialised work, he becomes exposed to these pressures as soon as he leaves the cloister and joins with others in the general cultural debate and endeavours to get practical policies adopted that are based upon his theoretical conclusions. It must often happen that unexpected incidents and temporary set-backs tempt him for the time being to doubt the force of arguments which would still seem to him sound if he were in a uniformly cool frame of mind. It is in this characteristically human predicament that faith is needed. A man may, of course, deliberately limit the range and scope of his decisions and live, so far as is practically possible, a thoroughly neutral and uncommitted life. Since most of the issues which engage the attention of his fellows are, in his view, unacceptably controversial, he prefers to be a non-voter and a non-participant. The danger is that by refusing to make explicit decisions in these controversial areas he will take over, in effect, the attitudes that prevail, at the time, in his particular milieu. He will not have much in the way of faith; but he is likely to have plenty of prejudices.

But in any case it is not clear that even the most cautious sceptic can avoid the tensions and temptations that I have been describing. His own parsimonious policy is based upon considerations of a broadly philosophical kind which are not shared by many of his colleagues and whose validity he must sometimes feel inclined to question; and he would be less than human if he were not strongly moved on occasions to break out of his narrow perimeter and throw in his lot with one or other of the contending parties beyond it. When assailed by such doubts he too requires the capacity to resist temptation.

My suggestion, then, is that there is a sense of 'faith' which is common to religious and secular contexts, and that faith in this sense need not be contrary to reason. Of course it can be. There are all too many examples, both secular and religious, of unthinking adherence to systems of belief which have little or no rational basis. And there are, and perhaps inevitably must be, innumerable cases of the comparatively unreflective acceptance of beliefs and attitudes, of whose rational basis those who accept them are largely unaware. The Socratic obligation λογον διδοναι is one which holds for intellectuals, but not everyone is obliged to be an intellectual.

It will, perhaps, be objected that I have assumed throughout (1) that a rational choice can, at least in principle, be made between 'philosophies of life' and (2) that a rational case can be made out for at least some religious 'philosophies of life'; and that both of these assumptions are, at best, controversial. This objection I am bound to admit, nor can I undertake to defend those assumptions within the limits of this article. The most I can do is to insist that they are, at least, controversial.

At this point I must turn to the question which I undertook to discuss at the beginning of my article, namely whether the faith of the religious believer is in all essentials equivalent to that of the adherent, explicit or implicit, of a non-religious philosophy of life who resists temptation to give it up when, in spite of his steady rational conviction in its favour, he encounters arguments and experiences which, logically or psychologically, threaten it. I am inclined to think that there is one important difference – at least where the religion in question is a theistic religion. Faith in God, for the Jew, the Christian or the Muslim, is not simply a commitment to a religious philosophy of life; it is a trusting reliance upon God. In this respect it is like faith in a person rather than like faith in some doctrine of human nature. As H. H. Price has pointed out,[3] if I have faith in my doctor this involves more than my believing that he exists and that he is what he purports to be, a qualified medical practitioner. It means that I rely upon him to care conscientiously for my health, to be honest in his dealings with me, and so on. The sort of faith I have been discussing so far would be analogous to my faith in modern medicine (as distinct from, say, African tribal medicine); and my faith in my doctor, though it presupposes this, is of a different order and goes well beyond it.

There can be no secular equivalent to faith in God in this sense since there is nothing that corresponds, in a secular scheme of things, to a personal God.

However, the existence of religious faith in this additional sense raises a serious question about the adequacy of my earlier discussion of faith in its religious application. Religious faith, it is commonly agreed, is, of its very nature, unconditional, whereas the sort of secular faith I have been discussing must, in the end, be in a certain sense tentative and provisional; it must in principle be open to revision and, in the last resort, rejection. This is involved in my characterisation of 'philosophies of life' as not unchallengeable. For when every allowance has been made for the need to adhere to a philosophy of life with a good deal of determination if it is to undergo adequate testing and provide the individual with 'a faith to live by', there may always come a point when the cumulative case against it becomes so strong that he ought to give it up. If there is no such point, then his faith is no longer based on reason at all but has turned into simply prejudice or sheer fanaticism. Either, then, the conception of religious faith as unconditional has to be rejected, in spite of its centrality in the tradition of the great theistic religions, or the attempt to reconcile faith and reason on the lines indicated earlier has to be abandoned.

One way in which to approach this problem is to stress the distinction between the two senses of faith and to claim that, when this is clearly recognised, the dilemma disappears. The faith that *is* unconditional is the believer's trust in God; it is this which forbids him to despair in the face of doubts and difficulties. This trust is the corollary of God's nature as he believes it to be. The God 'in whom is no variableness and shadow of turning' is a faithful and merciful God who will not abandon his creature. But it does not follow from this that the entire system of belief, including the belief that there is a God and that he is trustworthy, could not in the end turn out to be false. The unconditional trust in God which is called for within the theistic system cannot be construed as belief that the system itself is unquestionably true.

To this proposed solution it may be objected that, if this is so, the believer's faith is not religiously adequate: it cannot give him the reassurance he needs in face of the 'changes and chances of this transitory life'. As a psychological generalisation about religious believers, this is by no means obviously true. Some may crave logical guarantees of the truth of their beliefs; others may have no need of them. And, even if logical certainty were available, it could not, as a matter of psychology, be relied upon invariably to prevent the dryness of spirit in which even undoubted truths appear empty and unconsoling. If, on the other hand, the objection is not based upon psychology, but the contention is that the believer ought not to be reassured unless there is no possibility of his being proved wrong, it can be pointed out that, as things are, he may have good reasons for believing as he does, and sufficient reasons, along the lines of our previous discussion, for not allowing his beliefs continually to fluctuate.

I confess that I find it difficult to decide whether this reply is adequate or not. I once thought it was, but now I am not so sure. But I am inclined to think that this problem too is not confined to the religious case. There is a parallel in the sphere of personal relations in which certain accounts of the nature of human personality would, if accepted, seem to render irrational certain sorts of response towards people, to which men (or, at any rate, men in our culture) are deeply committed. The obvious example is the account given by B. F. Skinner, and the practical inferences drawn by him, in *Beyond Freedom and Dignity*.[4] It is hard to see how the unreserved openness and trust which most of us have and believe we ought to have towards our friends and our families could be justified in terms of Skinnerian psychology. How then should we react? Are we entitled to argue *from* our own intuitive conviction of the health and reasonableness of our personal responses *to* the evident falsity of Skinner's account? Must we deny, that is, that this account has any chance of proving true? Or should we conclude that, since Skinner could conceivably be right (though we do not personally believe he is), or some other account of human personality having similar implications could be right, we ought not to be as open and unreserved with those we love as we habitually are? That Skinner's view of human nature does indeed have these implications is, no doubt, open to some question, but it cannot be said to be beyond all reasonable doubt that it does not. In general it would be a bold man who was prepared to claim that there exists today any doctrine of human nature which commands universal assent among all reasonable men, or who was prepared to claim that it was beyond all reasonable doubt that our conception of what human beings are like has no implications for the way we should treat them. If this is so, the man who loves and trusts his intimates unreservedly is in a similar case to the one who has unconditional faith in God. Neither can nor should allow his personal responses to be affected by the possibility (which he acknowledges) that he could be wrong in some of his fundamental beliefs.

I said at the beginning of this article that I would end by saying a little about the educational implications of the problem we have been discussing. I noted that in the educational debate, especially in relation to religious education, it is often taken for granted that we have to choose between two alternatives: on the one hand, indoctrination; on the other an entirely open-ended or phenomenological approach. Indoctrination consists in the inculcation of received opinions; the open-ended approach seeks to encourage an attitude that is entirely critical and creative. When presented with these alternatives we have little option but to choose the latter, for 'indoctrination' is evidently not an educational procedure at all. Yet the ideal of an education that aims solely at the development of individuals who are critical and creative seems, on reflection, to be curiously vacuous. To be creative is, so far as it goes, good; but is it of no concern what is created? Criticism is to be encouraged, but upon what is the critical capacity to be exercised? Can the individual learn to be either critical or creative without first having been inducted into a continuing tradition of some kind? As R. S. Peters (one of the sanest of British educational theorists) writes:

> The emphasis on 'critical thinking' was salutary enough, perhaps, when bodies of knowledge were handed on without any attempt being made to hand on also the public procedures by which they had been accumulated, criticized and revised. But it is equally absurd to foster an abstract skill called 'critical thinking' without handing on anything concrete to be critical about.[5]

In talking, as he does here, of something concrete to be handed on Peters seems to be suggesting that there is a need for a continuing tradition upon which the individual can draw and to which he can make his own unique contribution. Given such a tradition – so long as it is a reasonable one, and this is an important qualification – there is room for criticism which may result in modifying the tradition or, indeed, rejecting it. Without some such tradition there is, arguably, no possibility of critical or creative thought at all. Nothing is more absurd than to suppose that the individual, however intelligent and industrious he is, can develop the whole of science or any other academic discipline or morality or religion from scratch. He must be prepared to accept authority in all these fields – in fact in respect of everything in which being civilised consists – as a necessary condition of becoming critical and creative in them.

If what I said earlier is correct, about the extent to which controversy is endemic in most academic disciplines and *a fortiori* in all philosophies of life, we cannot expect that any tradition in which, as educators, we stand, will be unchallengeable (although it may be largely unchallenged within a particular culture or intellectual milieu). No doubt there are large areas of factual information and common-sense belief which can be taken entirely for granted, but as soon as we penetrate at all deeply beyond these areas into subjects of serious intellectual study, we find ourselves in realms of more or less vigorous controversy. Hence, if anything concrete is to be handed on (to use Peters' words), it is likely to be something that can be controverted. There is a revealing phrase sometimes used by scholars describing their own student days: 'At Oxford (Princeton, Heidelberg) in my day we were *taught to believe* that . . . [metaphysics was impossible and that neither Aquinas nor Hegel were worth reading].' This does not generally mean that their teachers inculcated certain doctrines into them in such a way that they were subsequently unable to treat them critically; but rather that their teachers themselves accepted these doctrines, believed themselves to be justified in doing so, and, in the way they treated the subject, influenced the students so that they in turn largely accepted them. In this way the students became heirs to a recognisable philosophical tradition. But in so far as the teachers also taught them to be creative and critical (and in our Western universities they generally did), the latter were able to review in course of time what they had thus been 'taught to believe', and so the tradition developed. How to strike the balance between these two elements in the educational process is a practical question of some difficulty, but that a balance needs to be struck seems to me to be clear.

That this is so is most apparent in the case of the most profoundly critical and creative minds. Much literary and historical research consists in the attempt to uncover the 'influences' which made them what they were and, happily, such research seems always to leave a sheer unexplained leap of originality which it cannot account for. But what does emerge is the extent to which, characteristically, such minds have absorbed the best of the work of their predecessors. Some time ago a friend of mind was engaged in editing the correspondence between Holst and Vaughan Williams, and asked me to identify a quotation from Gilbert Murray which one of them had quoted with approbation to the other. I was somewhat daunted by the prospect of searching through Murray's voluminous writings, but the quotation was about genius and it occurred to me that a possible source, readily available to the general reader, was his little volume on Euripides in the Home University Library. And there, in the introduction, I found what I was looking for. It read:

Every man who possesses real vitality can be seen as the resultant of two forces. He is first the child of a particular age, society, convention; of what we may call in one word a tradition. He is secondly, in one degree or another, a rebel against that tradition. And the best traditions make the best rebels.[6]

Gilbert Murray, I suggest, gets the balance right. We have, as educators, to make our pupils heirs to a tradition in such a manner that, in due course, they are free to appropriate it, modify it, develop it or reject it. If we decline to do this, through fear of exerting undue influence upon them, they will not thereby be enabled to discover some genuinely original alternative of their own; they will simply absorb uncritically the current fashions of the day and make what they can of them. I have argued that a healthy tradition, whether secular or religious, calls for both faith and reason, and that there is an inevitable tension between them. Although in this lecture it is the faith that I have stressed, because, as it seems to me, the need for it is too often overlooked, I hold no brief for unreasoned prejudice. To return to Alice, it will not do to take the White Queen's advice 'Try again: draw a long breath and shut your eyes.'

10

PHILOSOPHY AND THEOLOGY*

In his *Philosophies and Cultures* Father Frederick Copleston has occasion from time to time to remark on the relationship between philosophy and theology at different periods and, where the comparison is appropriate, in different cultures.[1] Such reflections lead one naturally to consider what the relationship between them is, or should be, in our culture today.

It would be in the spirit of Father Copleston's own procedure to start not from abstract definitions but from actual practice. If one looks at degree syllabuses, for example at Oxford, philosophy and theology would appear to be very different. A student of theology engages for much of the time in the study of the Bible from a historical and critical point of view, and also of the languages in which it is written, especially Greek. In addition, he studies the Fathers and as much of the history of the Christian Church and of Christian doctrine as he can manage. Then there is Christian doctrine as a subject in its own right, together, perhaps, with some philosophy of religion. A student of philosophy studies logic and theory of knowledge, moral and political philosophy, with, perhaps, the philosophy of mind or the philosophy of language. To this is added a certain amount of the history of philosophy from Descartes to the present day, together with Greek and Latin, if ancient and medieval philosophy are included.

* From Gerard J. Hughes (ed.), *The Philosophical Assessment of Theology: Essays in Honour of Frederick C. Copleston* (Tunbridge Wells: Search Press and Georgetown University Press, 1987), pp. 3–14.

Apart from the history of philosophy – and even then to quite a large extent – the student of philosophy spends all his time actually philosophising. The differences in subject are differences in what he philosophises about. If by 'theology' we mean systematic theology, it is not true in the same way that the theologian spends most of his time theologising. Much of his work is a variety of literary or historical criticism, devoted to a strict study of the biblical text; and the same is true of patristics.

The contrast between the two disciplines is sharpened if one concentrates upon the 'rigorous core' of each subject – that part of it which undergraduates are required to do for the good of their souls when, often, they would rather be doing something else. In theology it is biblical criticism; in philosophy it is philosophical logic. Philosophical logic is basic to philosophy in that it concerns the philosophical analysis of key concepts, such as those of meaning and truth, which are involved in any kind of philosophy; and, when engaged in philosophical logic, one is, paradigmatically, philosophising. Biblical criticism is basic to theology, but in a recognisably different way. One can be a biblical critic without being a theologian at all.

By comparison with philosophy, theology looks like a collection of disparate disciplines. What, then, makes it a single subject? Taken as a whole, if one goes on the evidence of degree syllabuses, theology would seem to be identical with hermeneutics (in a broadly intelligible sense of that word), viz. with the attempt to answer the question 'What ought the Christian now to believe, given that the biblical writers and their successors in the Christian tradition believed what they did?' It is essential to the hermeneutical task, so understood, that the meaning of the original documents be ascertained as accurately as possible – hence the enormous investment in linguistic and historical study – but more than that is needed, since the theologian is concerned with what is to be believed today, and this is affected by much that we know now and was not known to the biblical writers.

On the face of it philosophy is not related in the same way to a set of foundation documents. A philosopher who read Greats at Oxford may feel that a philosopher who does not read Greek and has not studied Plato and Aristotle must be a rather ill-equipped philosopher, but he does not deny him the title of philosopher; and he himself does not feel inadequate because of his ignorance of, say, Aquinas or Hegel. *Some* acquaintance with the great philosophers of the past is necessary, but it need not be systematic or comprehensive. And the contemporary philosopher is, it would appear, in no way *committed*, *qua* philosopher, to the thought of any of his predecessors. If he is interested in Plato and impressed by him, he can practise hermeneutics upon him and endeavour to express certain key Platonic doctrines in terms that are acceptable today, but it is a task that is in no sense laid upon him. As a rule philosophers tend to distinguish between philosophical scholars, those concerned with the exegesis and interpretation of Plato, and philosophers proper, who are interested chiefly in whether what Plato said is true, and who are often content to treat him as if he were a contemporary and not to mind interpreting him anachronistically.

The contrast may, however, be somewhat overdrawn. As Father Copleston has pointed out,[2] in the ancient world, especially in the Hellenistic period, philosophy was looked upon as a guide to life, and to be a Stoic, Epicurean or Neoplatonist was to place oneself within a recognised tradition. It was only in the medieval period that theology superseded philosophy in that function. The modern analytic philosopher's absence of commitment may simply be a historical oddity. And even within this modern movement (as the word 'movement' itself suggests) it is possible to exaggerate the individual philosopher's degree of detachment. There exists a tacit, if informal, canon of historical and contemporary works with which he is expected to familiarise himself, and certain topics are to be taken more seriously than others. Moreover, even today a philosopher can identify himself with a tradition which goes back to a particular thinker. He may declare himself a Thomist or a Kantian or a Humean, convinced that these philosophers had the root of the matter in them and no less concerned to express the thought of these philosophers in contemporary terms than any practitioner of biblical hermeneutics.

Nor do all contemporary theologians conform to the pattern I have sketched. Professor Maurice Wiles has suggested in an Oxford seminar that all that is required of the theologian is that he should attend to 'the theological agenda'; he need not be committed in advance to any particular interpretation of it or to its defence. A possible example of such a theologian is Professor Dennis Nineham.[3] He is a New Testament critic who repudiates the hermeneutical task (in the sense I have given it) as impossible of fulfilment. The meaning of the New Testament writers is so bound up with the thought-forms of their age and so remote from anything we can understand, let alone believe today, that there is no point in trying to find an interpretation of it which can be made accessible to our contemporaries. We must endeavour to understand God in terms of modern categories alone, and be content to derive from the Bible and the rest of the Christian tradition only the assurance that a relationship with God can be sustained at any period, no matter how we conceive of him.

Nevertheless the existence of these variations from the norm is not enough to call the norm itself seriously in question. They are recognisably uncharacteristic. That this is so can be seen from the particular case of Marxism. Marxist thinkers are often classed with theologians rather than with philosophers, precisely because in their case it is not just that, as individual thinkers, they have found something to admire in a historical philosopher and chosen to develop his thought. They have associated themselves with a broad social and political movement which has its origins in the philosophy of this one thinker and which, in the Communist Party, possesses an organised institution, analogous to a Church, to which allegiance is owed. The movement is attended by such characteristically religious phenomena as conversion, apostasy and sectarianism. The attitude of Marxists to the works of Marx and Engels is closer to that of Christian theologians to the New Testament than is that of contemporary philosophers to any of their predecessors.

Having, provisionally at least, made these discriminations, let us now consider to what extent the theologian is or ought to be a philosopher. My initial suggestion is that much of what the systematic theologian does just *is* philosophy. He seeks to interpret the Christian tradition, and the biblical writers in particular, in such a way that they can be seen to provide answers to the major questions about life. That they can do so is a presupposition of the whole enterprise, as is the conviction of its existential relevance. How the process operates can best be seen in somewhat unorthodox theologians. Bultmann, for example, is concerned to interpret the significance of the New Testament for today. That it represents, or contains, fundamental truth he does not doubt. The question to be answered is: Under what interpretation can its message be both true and relevant to the modern world? Taken at its face value most of what it says must now be rejected as false, since it is bound up with a mythological view of the world which has been rendered obsolete by the development of modern science. It must, therefore, be demythologised and the original kerygma expressed in terms acceptable today, *viz.* in those of the philosophy of Heidegger.

Bultmann's procedure is philosophical throughout, and not only in his use of existentialist language. It is a *philosophical* assumption, derived perhaps from Kant, that modern science exhausts the realm of objective fact and that the world as we experience it is a closed nexus of cause and effect, within which God cannot be supposed to be active. It is by contrast with *this* that the world-view of the New Testament is held to be mythological. In his treatment of this 'mythological' language of the New Testament Bultmann relies upon a dichotomy, philosophical in character, between fact-stating and expressive uses of language. The mythology of the New Testament appears at first sight to be fact-stating but, so understood, it must stand condemned as obsolete science. Therefore it must not be so understood. That it might conceivably be both mythological (*i.e.*, metaphorical) *and* fact-stating is a possibility that Bultmann's philosophical assumptions do not allow him to entertain.

The philosophical character of Bultmann's procedure is apparent if we compare him with Professor D. Z. Phillips, who writes specifically as a philosopher. Phillips accepts from the New Testament, and from the Christian tradition as a whole, the doctrine of eternal life. Like Bultmann he is committed to holding that it is in some sense true. But, taken at its face value, it is obviously not true. Dead people stay dead, and we have learned from Hume that the notion of survival of bodily death is logically incoherent. Eternal life must therefore mean something else, and what it means, Phillips tells us in *Death and Immortality*, is that it is open to us now so to live as to render death irrelevant.[4]

The examples of Bultmann and Phillips may provoke the objection that the hermeneutical task, as they exemplify it, is not so much that of interpreting the Christian tradition as of radically reinterpreting it. If, in deference to philosophical principles, the theologian is forced to such extremes as these in order to discover in the Bible a message that can be received as true for us today, would it not be wiser and more honest, we may be inclined to say, to give up the attempt altogether? And this is what Nineham in effect does. There is *no* way of interpreting the message of the New Testament writers in terms that are acceptable today. Myth *and* kerygma are equally beyond recall. What the tradition preserves for us, and all that we can or need rely upon, is not a message at all but an institution, the Church, which is able to make available to believers today the same fullness of relationship with God as the primitive church experienced in the first century. In developing his argument Nineham relies heavily on another philosophical theory, a variety of conceptual relativism, which leads him to assert that, even if we could by an exercise of historical imagination come to have some inkling of what, for example, Paul meant, there is no possibility of our believing it today.

I have introduced this discussion of Bultmann and Phillips and Nineham in order to support the suggestion that, to a large extent, theologians *are* philosophers, with the tacit implication that other theologians less radical than they differ from them only in the sort of philosophy they employ or the use they put it to. But an entirely natural response to these examples would be to take them instead as illustrating the ill effects upon theology of tangling with philosophy at all. The proper lesson to be learned from them, it might be said, is that theologians should eschew philosophy and conduct their thinking throughout in purely biblical categories. This was, indeed, the programme of the Biblical Theology movement, which was largely a reaction against the tendency to identify the doctrines of Christianity with those of some preferred philosophical system, in particular Hegelian idealism (or worse still to regard them as provisional approximations to truths that had been finally revealed in Hegel). But however understandable that reaction was, it was bound eventually to encounter the hermeneutical problem, and with it the need to come to terms with philosophy. For what *were* the biblical concepts which were to be normative for theology? And how were they to be understood in a context different from that in which they had originated or developed? The concept of sin, for example, is central to Christianity as traditionally understood. Without it there is no need of salvation and no room for grace. But is it to be identified with ritual uncleanness or with moral wrongdoing or with something other than and more fundamental than either of these? How has it been related to moral responsibility at key points in the history of Christian doctrine (*e.g.*, in the thought of Augustine and Aquinas); and to what extent do current developments in psychology and sociology require that relationship to be understood differently today? To answer the historical questions demands all the resources of literary and historical scholarship, together with a critical study of these thinkers in their philosophical context. To answer the contemporary ones calls for familiarity with moral philosophy and the philosophy of mind.

Philosophy enters in also at a further remove from the present discussion. The hermeneutical task, as I have represented it, presupposes an essential continuity in the Christian tradition. The theologian, as he engages in it, is trying to express in contemporary terms truths which were first enunciated in the past in languages different from our own and in terms of different views of the world. It is, as we have seen, Nineham's conviction that this can scarcely be done, but, even if this extreme view is rejected, it remains clear that some defensible theory is needed of the continuity or development of doctrine. There is, that is to say, a philosophical problem of the identity of doctrine as between successive historical periods, which bears some resemblance to the familiar problem of personal identity. (Nineham adopts in relation to it something very much like Hume's scepticism about the self.) Philosophers have paid little attention to it because they are not themselves, as a rule, concerned to maintain an unbroken historical tradition; but it is a philosophical problem nevertheless.

If, as the argument suggests, a theologian is bound to be for much of the time, whether he likes it or not, a philosopher, what other equipment does he need? Would the best way to get a good theologian be to take a good philosopher and set him to work on the 'theological agenda'? Not unless he also receives the training needed to enable him to cope competently with that agenda, which involves being well grounded in the disciplines mentioned earlier as comprising the theological syllabus: the critical study of the Bible, patristics, the history of Christian doctrine, and so on.

Suppose him, however, to have been through all this successfully, will he now *be* a theologian? This is a question to be answered to some extent by stipulation. One may wish to stipulate, as Wiles does, that so long as he directs his attention to the 'theological agenda' and forms some conclusions about it, making use of the theological skills he has developed, then he is a theologian, no matter what those conclusions are. He may have reached largely sceptical conclusions about the historicity of the Gospels, decided that the Fathers were preoccupied with philosophical distinctions that are now entirely obsolete, and been persuaded by Hume and modern

Humeans that the concept of God is logically incoherent. There would, then, be no point in him trying to interpret the Christian message in terms intelligible and acceptable today. The most that he could offer in this direction would be to do his best for Christianity, to allow it the benefit of the doubt in certain important respects and, by an effort of sympathetic imagination, to state its contentions as persuasively as he can. It sometimes happens that atheistic philosophers do this very well – one thinks of J. L. Mackie's treatment of theological ethics[5] – but it is, nevertheless, an essentially parasitic activity, which would not be engaged in unless there were others who actually believed in what they were doing. Hence Wiles' stipulative definition has at best only a secondary use, and it is these latter thinkers who, standing within the tradition and concerned to explicate and defend its fundamental truths, are to be regarded as theologians properly so-called.

The theologian, then, the argument so far suggests, is a philosopher, with the requisite training in the other disciplines needed, who addresses himself to the hermeneutical task. In so doing he will not expect to find total coherence and completeness in the tradition but as much coherence and completeness as is needed in order to understand and appropriate the Christian scheme of salvation. This means giving sufficient weight both to the historical texts and to the contemporary constraints upon belief. The sort of balance demanded can best be seen by considering extreme cases of the failure to achieve it. Fundamentalism fails because it is insufficiently critical in its approach to the Bible; it ignores or denies the relevance of what can be discovered by rational methods about the language and historical context of the biblical writers and the meaning of what they wrote. Radicalism often fails because it is equally uncritical of what passes for modern knowledge, assuming too readily that, where there is some conflict between the Christian tradition and what is accepted as true by contemporary secular intellectuals, it is the former that must give way. The hermeneutical task, which I have taken as central to theology, involves interpreting the biblical message in terms that are, so far as possible, intelligible and defensible today, but this does not mean 'in terms that are already understood and accepted today', quite independently of the Christian tradition. The theological task presupposes – and this was the truth in the Biblical Theology movement – that the dominant concepts of the Christian tradition do actually possess an enduring power to interpret and illuminate human experience. It follows that, when they are confronted with other conceptual systems which we have some warrant for accepting on scientific or philosophical grounds, some modification is to be expected on one side or the other or on both. To return to the example used earlier, that of the theological concept of sin, considerable light may be cast on it by the Freudian doctrine of the unconscious, but it would be rash for the theologian simply to identify sin with the unconscious. Modern psychology may dictate greater caution in attributing guilt than was customary in past ages, but contemporary notions of guilt may themselves be judged superficial when contrasted with the Christian understanding of sin. If the tradition possesses the sort of intellectual vitality which is presupposed by the practice of theology, it will exhibit this capacity for reciprocal interaction with secular trends without, however, being entirely exhaustible by them. A possible analogy, though a controversial one, is with the production of Shakespeare's plays. A creative director will discover in Shakespeare contemporary resonances which, it is reasonable to suppose, would not have been present to the minds of his original audience. Given today's obsession with sex and violence, they may well have to do with these. Shakespeare's inexhaustibility is such that a reciprocal movement actually occurs. We are led to discover more in Shakespeare than we realised was there; and our current preoccupation with sex and violence is given an extra dimension of meaning. This is what a good director will achieve. A poor director may instead end up by imposing upon Shakespeare's play a fashionable and wholly ephemeral interpretation which succeeds only in depriving it of much of its original significance. He will have interposed his own personality with its transitory interests between his audience and Shakespeare, whereas the other had enabled Shakespeare to engage and enlarge our contemporary vision.

If a process of this kind occurs when our theologically equipped philosopher turns to systematic theology, it will follow that in bringing his philosophy to bear on the 'theological agenda' he is not just using philosophical methods or applying philosophical conclusions which have answered well in other branches of philosophy. It is a well-worn theme in the philosophy of religion that meanings require to be stretched when terms are applied to God that have their regular use in other contexts – and all theological terms bear some relationship to God. So it will not do for the philosopher to argue, for example, that, because our ordinary concept of causality cannot be applied to God, there can be no concept of causality applicable to God; or that, since some concept of causality is applicable to God, and this is the only concept available, this must be the one that is applicable to God. Philosophers and theologians are constantly tempted in one or other of these directions. Of course it may turn out, in a particular instance, that no stretching is needed, but the presumption must always be otherwise.

But how is the theologian to tell what modifications are needed among all those that would achieve consistency, and what sort of reasoning does he employ in reaching a decision? What warrant, indeed, has he for accepting, in the first instance, the basic assumption which I have taken to be essential to the practice of theology, *viz.* that it is possible to identify and interpret the teaching of the Bible so that it is intelligible and acceptable today? An objector might complain that, according to my account, the theologian has *carte blanche* to reach any conclusions he likes, for it can only be a matter of subjective judgement how a particular individual achieves the balance I have argued for.

Personal judgement no doubt, but by no means purely subjective. The theologian's judgement is constrained by all the disciplines that are relevant to his task. He has, for instance, to run the gauntlet of biblical criticism (or give adequate reason why he should not). I have talked hitherto somewhat vaguely, as if using an admissible shorthand, about 'the biblical message', but it is a commonplace of biblical criticism that, even if we confine ourselves to the New Testament, the different writers have their characteristic points of view, and leading individuals like Paul do not always speak with one voice. In the patristic period and later the diversity of voices is influenced by philosophical and political considerations of an arguably extraneous kind. With the Reformation even the formal unity of the Western Church is no longer maintained and, after the Enlightenment, reason and religion are increasingly at odds. At each stage the theologian is confronted by a chorus of 'buts'. 'But the New Testament has no unified doctrine.' 'But the doctrine of the Trinity owes more to Greek philosophy and imperial policy than to the New Testament.' 'But the theology of the Reformation resists all attempts to found faith on reason.' These have either to be rebutted or accepted in whole or in part; they cannot simply be ignored, and reasons have to be given for the line that is eventually taken. In no case is it enough for the theologian simply to legislate. There are linguistic, historical, philosophical and other considerations to be assessed on their merits. These are not entirely determinate, but neither is the theologian free to decide them just as he wishes. The range of possible meanings of a Greek expression as used in the first century AD is limited, and the views of reputable scholars have to be respected. One cannot simply choose to override them. But it may on occasion be legitimate to employ some later usage as a clue to what was originally meant, if the context will bear it. When a single individual says one thing at one time and another later, it is a reasonable procedure to look for an interpretation of both utterances which will render them consistent. A principle of charity operates – a writer is presumed to be consistent unless it is clear that he is not. And if a reading that is slightly less probable on the other available evidence would render him consistent, there is reason to prefer it. If consistency cannot be saved at all, or only at the cost of undue special pleading, it is reasonable to ask which of the alternatives best coheres with the author's overall view, and what this is has to be determined on the evidence of these and other relevant passages. Here again charity dictates that, *ceteris paribus*, one prefer the view that makes the better sense.

Where a number of people are linked as a group, formally or informally, in maintaining an overall position, and they sometimes differ, an analogous situation arises, but only analogous. That A and B, who are associated in some way, should nevertheless have independent views which may conflict, is not surprising, so that one cannot invoke the principle of charity to quite the same effect. Yet, if they do agree considerably in fact, and if they see themselves as part of the same movement, it makes sense to try to reconcile their divergent utterances so far as possible and to look for common assumptions that underlie them. Moreover there is the possibility, even the likelihood, that they are trying to get at the same basic contention without entirely succeeding. There is a possible instance of this in Sir Alfred Ayer's televised conversation with Bryan Magee where, after admitting that most of what the Logical Positivists said was false, he went on, 'Nevertheless, I think the approach was right.'[6] Here was a loosely defined group of philosophers who undoubtedly had certain important assumptions in common and who often disagreed with one another on particular points. Yet they were all looking for a formula which would distinguish definitively between science and metaphysics and so enable them to dispose finally of the claims of theology. If there had existed such a formula, it is entirely possible that many of their differing utterances could plausibly have been construed as inadequate and approximate attempts to articulate it.

The Logical Positivists were contemporaries, but in many respects they were the philosophical heirs of David Hume. It would not be wholly misleading to describe them as endeavouring to bring Hume up to date. They illustrate, then, the tendency already alluded to, for philosophical doctrines to have histories which endure through several generations. Such doctrines characteristically offer solutions to enduring problems of a kind that require more than a single lifetime to explore. It is to be expected, on this ground alone, that the same should be true of theological doctrines whose transcendent subject-matter precludes definitive interpretation.

Along these lines I should want to argue that the presumption underlying the theological enterprise is defensible – that it is, in principle, possible to identify and interpret the biblical message in such a way as to render it intelligible and acceptable today. It is entirely compatible with this claim that the history of Christian doctrine should be one of dilution and corruption as well as of reform and regeneration. What is needed to validate the use of this model of continuing identity is not that change and controversy should be absent, but the persistence of a recognisable something of which one can intelligibly say that it has been diluted and corrupted, reformed and regenerated.

The words 'in principle' often betray the philosopher at work, and it is arguable that they mark the boundaries of philosophical involvement in theology. No doubt it is appropriate for the philosopher to draw attention to the kind of identity through time that a doctrinal tradition might possess and to suggest the criteria that need to be satisfied for a particular claim to be made good. More generally, it is for the philosopher to distinguish and elucidate the conceptual possibilities between which a choice has to be made. 'Does God act in the world or reveal himself in the words of prophets and evangelists?' The philosopher can assist the theologian by offering alternative ways of explicating the concepts of 'divine action' and 'revelation' respectively, perhaps showing that there are more, and more fertile, possibilities available than the theologian had previously thought. But eventually the theologian has to decide not just whether 'in principle' God could have acted or revealed himself, but when and how he did so – given the Judaeo-Christian tradition and anything else that may be relevant. To be able to do this he has to draw not only on the specific capacities of a linguistic, literary and historical kind which are developed by a theological education, but also on a broader capacity to interpret and weigh the various types of specialised evidence in order to achieve an overall account which is theologically illuminating and rationally defensible. The requirement that it be rationally defensible means that the exercise of philosophy is not, so to speak, actually transcended at this stage. Philosophical criticisms would still remain in place, and meeting them would be a philosophical exercise, but the total activity of the systematic theologian would seem to demand qualities of imagination and judgement in spiritual matters which do not belong to philosophy as such.

And yet, if a thoroughly prepared adversary were to go through the argument, step by step, contesting some or all of the specialist moves and concluding, for reasons given, that the cumulative case the theologian had developed and sought to defend was less persuasive than an ultimately atheistic interpretation of the entire 'theological agenda', what else could we call him but a philosopher or a metaphysician? Which seems to make the systematic theologian a philosopher and a metaphysician too. But not only that, for the theologian has put forward a coherent interpretation of the world, informed by a tradition to which he stands committed and which presupposes certain spiritual realities and calls for spiritual discernment. Neither the commitment nor the discernment belong to him *qua* philosopher. The philosophical critic's systematic rebuttal of Christian claims takes the form it does, of a re-ordering of the 'theological agenda', only because there already exists a continuing tradition of Christian thinkers committed to the hermeneutical task.

11

HOW TO PLAY THEOLOGICAL PING-PONG*

I must first apologise for the frivolity of my title, and the frivolity of my paper, which it all too faithfully reflects. It perhaps only makes it worse that they are serious topics that I am treating frivolously.

An Introduction to the Basic Rules of the Game

As a philosopher newly venturing into the field of theology I discern, or fancy that I discern, a certain recurrent pattern which those more familiar with it may no longer perceive quite so clearly. It is a pattern which is exemplified in passages such as this. The writer is Bultmann, in his reply to Schniewind. Since it is the pattern which I am interested in, I do not propose to describe the context, which will, however, emerge clearly enough.

> To point to the revelation as the only solution to the dilemma is to labour from the outset under a false assumption about the answer of revelation to the question of faith, and to substitute a *Weltanschauung* for faith. The question which faith asks is quite different from that asked by philosophy or by the natural sciences. And conversely, the revelation of God in Christ gives no answer whatever to the questions asked by philosophy and the natural sciences.[1]

* Originally read to 'Theological Wine', an informal theological group in Oxford, *c.* 1970.

And again later:

> True it is impossible to prove that faith is related to its object. But . . . it is just here that its strength lies. For if it were susceptible to proof it would mean that we could know and establish God apart from faith, and that would be placing him on a level with the world of tangible, objective reality.[2]

Then again Bultmann complains that Schniewind

> is liable to obscure the eschatological character of the Christian faith in revelation, and to make that revelation a *revelatum*, something which took place in the past and is now an object of detached observation, and the kerygma a bare report about something now dead and done with. And that is to forget that 'now is the day of salvation'.[3]

A similar pattern, displayed in relation to the same subject-matter, is to be found in H. Richard Niebuhr, *The Meaning of Revelation*. He also attacks the notion of revelation as something given (Bultmann's *revelatum*). He calls it a 'possessed revelation'.

> Such possessed revelation must be a static thing and under the human control of the Christian community – a book, a creed, or a set of doctrines. It cannot be a revelation in act whereby the church itself is convicted of its poverty, its sin and misery before God. Furthermore it cannot be the revelation of a living God: for the God of a revelation that can be possessed must be a God of the past, a God of the dead . . .[4]

Finally the pattern emerges in a single sentence from Richard Niebuhr.

> The strange question whether the same statement can be true in philosophy and untrue in theology, or *vice versa*, can no longer arise, for the reason that the statement as it occurs in the one can find no place in the other and, alike as they may sound, their difference must always be presupposed.[5]

In these passages what Bultmann and Niebuhr both do is to set up a dramatic contrast between two possible positions. *Either* revelation is something which occurred in the past, a possible object of detached contemplation, to be found in a book, a creed, or a set of doctrines, *or* it is a revelation in act, it has an eschatological character; *either* it is a bare report about something dead and done with, revealing 'A God of the past, a God of the *dead*,' *or* 'It is a revelation of the *living* God', and *now* is the day of salvation'.

The pattern to which I want to call attention is a very simple one. It is assumed that the question at issue permits of two and only two answers; between them they exhaust the field and they are mutually exclusive. The problem having been set up in this way the author can proceed, as in the passages quoted, to point out the absurdity of one of the alternatives, thus vindicating the other without having to produce any positive argument in its favour; or, as we shall see later, he may employ more subtle gambits.

To talk of 'gambits' suggests a game; and the pattern I have outlined does call to mind a party game invented by the art historian Sir Ernst Gombrich. Of this game he says:

> It consists of creating the simplest imaginable medium in which relationships can still be expressed, a language of two words only – let us call them 'ping' and 'pong'. If these were all we had and we had to name an elephant and a cat, which would be 'ping' and which 'pong'? I think the answer is clear. Or hot soup and ice cream. To me at least ice cream is ping and soup pong. Or Rembrandt and Watteau? Surely in that case Rembrandt would be pong and Watteau ping. I do not maintain that it always works, that two values are sufficient to categorize all relationships. We find people differing about day and night and male and female but perhaps these different answers could be reduced to un-ambiguity if the questions were differently framed. Pretty girls are ping and matrons pong. It may depend on which aspect of womanhood the person has in mind, just as the motherly, enveloping aspect of night is pong, but its

sharp, cold and menacing physiognomy may be ping to some.[6]

Gombrich's game of ping-pong is in one respect more general and in another more specific than the theological ping-pong I am interested in. It is more general in that ping and pong are adjectives of the widest possible generality, capable of being applied to any subject-matter whatever; more specific in that only one operation is called for, namely that of classifying a given pair of things as either ping or pong. Theological ping-pong, as I conceive it, consists in stating two alternative positions in relation to a particular issue with the stipulation or the assumption that one or the other of them is true but not both. The combinations that are ruled out by the conventions of the game are:

1. '*Neither* ping *nor* pong';
2. '*Both* ping *and* pong'.

Theological ping-pong, so understood, does of course admit as a sub-species a Gombrich-type procedure of classification, in which various abstract terms are substituted for ping and pong. I do not wish to dilate upon this particular sub-species, only to note in passing that Tillich is a past master of it, as he is of every kind of theological ping-pong.

For example, in his *Theology of Culture*, which is a very rich mine of examples, he begins chapter two by asserting that there are two possible types of philosophy of religion: the ontological type and the cosmological type. The game, then, is how to allocate particular philosophers between them, which Tillich has no difficulty in doing. In chapter three ping and pong are represented by time and space and Tillich puts on a virtuoso performance by classifying religions as either spatial or temporal. Thus he suggests that paganism can be defined as the elevation of a special space to ultimate value and dignity. Paganism, he says, has a god who is bound to one place beside and against other places. Similarly modern nationalism is a religion of space. By contrast, the Jewish prophets achieved a religion of time and not of space. For the prophets the God of time is the God of history. In this way Tillich is able to weave into his pattern another familiar contrast – between Hellenistic and Hebraic – for 'the power of space was overwhelming in Greek mind and existence'.[7]

In this instance I find that Tillich achieves some genuine illumination, but by the end of the book one has become somewhat sceptical as to the means by which it has been done. For by this time one has, so to speak, been bombarded with ping-pong balls. A hasty re-reading reveals the following dichotomies in addition to cosmological/ontological and spatial/temporal:

nominalism/realism;
existential/theoretical;
sacred/secular;
symbol/sign;
essence/existence;
moral/morality;
theonomy/heteronomy;
naturalism/supranaturalism;
inducting education/humanist education.

Clearly Tillich deserves a study to himself, but space does not allow, and it is time to return to my main theme.

The initial conventions of the game are, as has been explained, that two combinations are ruled out:

1. '*Neither* ping *nor* pong';
2. '*Both* ping *and* pong'.

The object of the game is to establish your own position with the minimum trouble to yourself and the maximum discomfiture to your opponent, and the simplest and in normal circumstances the most straightforward way of doing this is by arguing as follows:

1. *Either* ping *or* pong;
2. *Not* pong;
3. Therefore ping.

This is how Bultmann and Richard Niebuhr proceed in the passages I began by quoting. Revelation, they both, in effect, argue, is *either* (ping) a relationship here and now with the living God *or* (pong) a bare report in historical documents about something dead and done with. That it is the latter no one can seriously maintain (not pong). Therefore it is the former (ping).

In a case like this the safest plan for the opponent is to refuse to play the game, however much such refusal may expose him to charges of lack of sportsmanship. Here is Austin Farrer, declining to play the game with Bultmann in a characteristically graceful manner:

> Bultmann insists that the divine in Christ can be acknowledged in our present existence only, and never revealed by historical research; and there is a sense in which that is true. The techniques of historical scholarship cannot establish that God lived in man, but only that certain things were done and certain words were said. But of course the work of historical scholarship may bring me face to face with what will awaken faith in me. Suppose I am historically persuaded that Christ preached himself as Son of God in the words of the Gospel, I may believe Christ then and there, and without waiting to hear Dr Bultmann preach him to me from the pulpit. Or again, if I did hear Dr Bultmann proclaiming the faith of the Church, I might not believe him until I had had leisure to search the Scriptures. What turned the scales might be the historical persuasion that the seeds of the Church's faith were not only in the Gospels but in the historical fact behind the Gospels.[8]

In other words, Farrer argues, '*both* ping *and* pong' (and '*not* ping *without* pong').

Another straightforward example of theological ping-pong in a different field is provided by Joseph Fletcher in his book *Situation Ethics*. It is not, I think, unfair to Fletcher to maintain that the entire argument of this book is of the form indicated, with 'legalism' and 'situationism' as the values of 'ping' and 'pong': *either* one is a legalist *or* one is a situationist. No reasonable man could be a legalist, or at least no reasonable man who embraces 'the genius or ethos or style of life of American culture and of the techno-scientific era'. Therefore one must be a situationist.

The 'legalist', as represented by Fletcher, holds the following beliefs.

1. That there exist absolute moral rules, which may never be broken.

2. That even in those cases in which a moral rule may be broken, there remains an element of evil in the situation; if it is broken, the evil may be excused but not eliminated.

3. That moral rules are, in some sense, 'given' or 'objective'.

4. That there are some moral rules which are universal in the sense of being recognised by all men.

5. That moral decisions can be 'prefabricated'.

Anyone who is unwilling to accept this conjunction of beliefs about moral rules has, it would seem, no alternative but to adopt Fletcher's view that 'moral rules are mere "maxims" which in any situation can be not only overridden but totally superseded by love'. 'All else,' he says, 'all other generalities (*e.g.*, "one should tell the truth", "one should respect life"), are at most only *maxims*, never rules. For the situationist there are no rules – none at all.' 'If a lie is told unlovingly it is wrong, evil; if it is told in love it is good, right.' It is legalistic, he tells us, to ask such questions as 'Is it right to have pre-marital intercourse, gamble, steal, abort, lie, defraud, break contracts, *et cetera*, *ad nauseam*.'[9]

Fletcher, it will be apparent, is a ping-pong player of immense zest and enthusiasm, but rather little subtlety of style. He is exposed to two serious dangers. The first is that it is altogether too evident that his opponent need not play the game. Unlike Tillich, who generally takes care to make his values for ping and pong extremely vague, Fletcher has made his account of legalism excessively specific; indeed he seems to be much clearer about what legalism is than he is about situationism. So long as one rejects any one of the tenets of legalism one is no longer a legalist, but it is quite evident that one does not thereby become a situationist. Hence '*neither* ping *nor* pong' is a very obvious possibility. And even if legalism is identified with only the first tenet on the list, that is with the claim that there are absolute moral rules which may never be broken, it is clear enough that a person might believe in moral rules which hold only *ceteris paribus*, that is to say so long as the agent was not faced with other, more stringent, obligations.

The second danger is that of counter-attack. The legalist has only to find some flaws in situationism, which is not very difficult to do, and by parity of reasoning he can argue '*not* pong and *therefore* ping'. The reader may be tempted to become a legalist of the most inflexible kind, if persuaded by Fletcher that the only alternative is to be a situationist.

So far I have been dealing with one, entirely straight-forward, way of playing theological ping-pong. I want next to consider some more refined gambits.

More Advanced Strategies

1 *Transcending ping and pong*

This consists in maintaining that the truth lies neither in ping nor in pong, but *transcends* both ping and pong. For an exponent of this approach we can scarcely do better than return to Tillich, who, on his day, is a performer of unrivalled skill. Indeed it is doubtful if theological ping-pong has ever presented a more dazzling spectacle than Tillich transcending. My quotation comes, once again, from his *Theology of Culture*, where Tillich is giving, in the introductory chapter, a summary of his philosophical theology:

> If you start with the question whether God does or does not exist, you can never reach Him; and if you assert that He does exist, you can reach him even less than if you assert that He does not exist. A God about whose existence or non-existence you can argue is a thing beside others within the universe of existing things. And the question is quite justified whether such a thing does exist, and the answer is equally justified that it does not exist. It is regrettable that scientists believe that they have refuted religion when they rightly have shown that there is no evidence whatsoever for the assumption that such a being exists. Actually, they have not only not refuted religion, but they have done it a

considerable service. They have forced it to reconsider and to restate the meaning of the tremendous word *God*.[10]

Theism is ping, atheism pong; and the truth, known to Tillich, transcends both of them.

What is this truth? It is that religion is the aspect of depth in the totality of human spirit.

> What does the metaphor of *depth* mean? It means that the religious aspect points to that which is ultimate, infinite, unconditional in man's spiritual life. Religion, in the largest and most basic sense of the word, is ultimate concern. And ultimate concern is manifest in all creative functions of the human spirit. It is manifest in the moral sphere as the unconditional seriousness of the moral demand. Therefore, if someone rejects religion in the name of the moral function of the human spirit, he rejects religion in the name of religion. Ultimate concern is manifest in the realm of knowledge as the passionate longing for ultimate reality. Therefore, if anyone rejects religion in the name of the 'cognitive function' of the human spirit, he rejects religion in the name of religion. Ultimate concern is manifest in the aesthetic function as the infinite desire to express ultimate meaning. Therefore, if anyone rejects religion in the name of the aesthetic function of the human spirit, he rejects religion in the name of religion. You cannot reject religion with ultimate seriousness, because ultimate seriousness, or the state of being ultimately concerned, is itself religion.[11]

Having wrong-footed any conceivable opponent, Tillich takes game, set and match.

When the excitement has died down, it may be wondered whether Tillich has obeyed the rules, according to which the combinations '*neither* ping *nor* pong' and '*both* ping *and* pong', are not permitted. Tillich would plead, and I think with sufficient justification, that in his view there is an element of truth in both ping and pong, as well as a great deal of falsehood, and that on the same level (so to speak) as ping and pong, there is something to be said for each against the other.

The truth is not some third alternative to theism and atheism in the same universe of discourse as theirs, nor is it some compromise between them; it is that which theism and atheism are both trying to say, but never succeed in saying until Tillich enables them to transcend both theism and atheism.

After observing Tillich at his bewitching best it would be an anticlimax to look for any other examples of transcendence. I therefore turn to the next gambit.

2 Holding ping and pong in dialectical tension

Here is Reinhold Niebuhr, in the first volume of his Gifford Lectures, holding in dialectical tension man's responsibility for sin on the one hand and the inevitability of sin on the other:

> The Christian doctrine of original sin, with its seemingly contradictory assertions about the inevitability of sin and man's responsibility for sin, is a dialectical truth which does justice to the fact that man's self-love and self-centredness are inevitable, but not in such a way as to fit into the category of natural necessity. It is within and by his freedom that man sins. The final paradox is that the discovery of the inevitability of sin is man's highest assertion of freedom.[12]

The way Niebuhr expresses himself in this particular passage may leave some doubt as to whether it *is* a genuine case of dialectical tension. For if sin is inevitable, but not by natural necessity, this *could* be a sort of inevitability that is entirely compatible with man's responsibility. And then what we should have would not be a case of 'neither ping-nor-pong-but-ping-and-pong-in-dialectical-tension' but simply a denial that ping and pong are exclusive alternatives.

But the context makes clear that this interpretation is wrong. For Niebuhr has already insisted that, when properly formulated,

> the doctrine remains absurd from the standpoint of a pure rationalism, for it expresses a relation between fate and

freedom which cannot be fully rationalized, unless the paradox be accepted as a rational understanding of the limits of rationality and as an expression of faith that a rationally irresolvable contradiction may point to a truth which logic cannot contain.[13]

This, I think, forbids us to interpret Niebuhr's position in such a way as not to involve 'a rationally irresolvable contradiction'.

If there is any remaining doubt it should be removed by his appeal to Kierkegaard (a generous acknowledgement by a great player of an even greater):

Kierkegaard's explanation of the dialectical relation of freedom and fate in sin is one of the profoundest in Christian thought. He writes: 'The concept of sin and guilt does not emerge in its profoundest sense in paganism. If it did paganism would be destroyed by the contradiction that man becomes guilty by fate . . . Christianity is born in this very contradiction. The concept of sin and guilt presupposes the individual as individual. There is no concern for his relation to any cosmic or past totality. The only concern is that he is guilty; and yet he is supposed to become guilty through fate, the very fate about which there is no concern. And thereby he becomes something which resolves the concept of fate, and to become that through fate! If this contradiction is wrongly understood it leads to false concepts of original sin. Rightly understood it leads to a true concept, to the idea namely that every individual is itself and the race and that the later individual is not significantly differentiated from the first man. In the possibility of anxiety freedom is lost, for it is overwhelmed by fate. Yet now it arises in reality but with the explanation that it has become guilty.'[14]

A display like this is guaranteed to demoralise any but the most resolute and resourceful opponent.

There are hints in this passage of Kierkegaard's of the possibility of another gambit which subsequent writers have exploited to effect. This is to declare that, in spite of all appearances to the contrary, when properly understood, ping *is* pong.

3 *Ping is pong*

Kierkegaard anticipates this move when he remarks, in passing, that 'every individual is itself *and* the race and that the later individual is not significantly differentiated from the first man'. My example, however, is drawn from W. G. Maclagan's *The Theological Frontier of Ethics*, in which he is examining a problem related to the one that troubled Niebuhr, namely, the relation between divine grace and human freedom. Morality presupposes responsibility, religion demands grace. On the face of it the two are incompatible. Niebuhr, in these circumstances, would have kept the two in dialectical tension. Maclagan has no use for this:

> What I find I cannot wonder is whether what is involved in the very conception of . . . freedom might not perhaps be negated without the freedom itself being negated also. To suppose that possible is (what else can I say?) to suppose not mystery, but nonsense; and a theology is worth no man's attention that does not submit itself to the same rigorous conditions of self-consistency and good sense as apply to every other reflective activity.[15]

What he does is first of all to narrow the problem down to the validity of the prayer for grace, in which men ask that their will be conformed to God's will and 'enabled'. This is, in fact, the only sort of prayer which he feels to be justified, and it is in answer to this prayer, if anywhere, that God's grace must be supposed to be at work. He is willing to countenance a conception of divine grace formed by analogy with one person being helped or influenced by another; but he insists that such help must always be 'environmental', never 'constitutive', *i.e.* it may take the form of encouragement, stimulus and support; but it cannot play any part in the individual's moral effort which alone makes the action 'his'.

So, I find myself confronted by these alternatives: either I must retract the denial of the possibility of constitutive grace, notwithstanding everything I have said on that subject; or else I must hold that, contrary to appearances, the prayer for enablement can be interpreted in terms consistent with that denial. Of these alternatives I adopt the second.[16]

This, then, is how he does it:

If we are to escape admitting the constitutive operation of grace without at the same time denying what can be described as the *substantial* validity of the prayer for enablement, we must deny that the essential character of that prayer is properly represented by its petitionary form. And this . . . is just what I should do. As the prayer for forgiveness is the act and expression of contrition, of moral recovery, so, I hold, what appears as petition for grace to make the resolution requested of us *is in fact itself the moral victory*, itself the resolution for which it seems to ask.[17]

In other words, in praying for grace we are at one and the same time manifesting the highest expression of human freedom and exhibiting the grace of God at work, because the grace of God *is to be identified with* the highest expression of human freedom: 'ping *is* pong'.

Maclagan is, perhaps, to be regarded as a philosopher rather than a theologian, but parallels could, I think, be found in others who are without qualification theologians. One thinks of John Baillie in *The Sense of the Presence of God* resolving the tension between faith and experience by claiming that the proper name of religious experience *is* faith.[18]

4 Other possibilities

I ought, perhaps, to make it clear that I do not imagine myself to have noticed every possible way of playing theological ping-pong. A game is always capable of being modified by the practice of creative players, and in such cases is not a static thing; it is only in retrospect that one can be sure of what was happening at the time. I have an uneasy feeling, for example, that that notably elusive performer Ian Ramsey may be playing a sort of ping-pong in the following passage, which occurs at the end of *Religious Language*. He is talking about episcopacy. Hooker, he explains, 'not only fails to recognize that "Episcopacy" may behave in two logically different ways, but does not notice at all that particular kind of logical behaviour which is, and most appropriately, odd'.[19]

> That which some claim is of the *esse* of the Church is (we may say) 'Episcopacy' with a capital E, such a word as is a kinsman of 'God,' one whose logical placing is as complex as that. Here we have what might be called theological Episcopacy. On the other hand, that which others claim is of the *bene esse* of the Church – what we may call 'small e' episcopacy or empirical episcopacy – is episcopacy known in terms of prelacy, bishops' stipends, reunion schemes, Church Commissioners and the rest. Here (we might say) is observable episcopacy.[20]

Here, then, we could perhaps find ping and pong, in the form of 'theological episcopacy' and 'empirical episcopacy'.

Ramsey continues:

> But these are two logical areas, which will only be bridged when stories about the latter can be so developed as to evoke a specifically Christian disclosure in relation to which alone theological Episcopacy can be commended. In this connection we can see the importance of a recent book which claims that Episcopacy is of the *plene esse* of the Church. For we may say that such a view (a) recognizes implicitly, if not explicitly, the double logical status of 'episcopacy,' and (b) tries to unite these two logical values by means of the model of 'filling' developed within a historical background.[21]

I am not sure that I know what game Ian Ramsey is playing here, but it is obviously a variety of ping-pong.

Advice to Novice Players

So far this has been a purely theoretical study, but you may reasonably expect me to make some suggestions as to how we should advise young theologians who have as yet little experience of playing this game. What are the advantages and disadvantages of the various gambits I have discussed, bearing in mind that the game is not solely or even mainly an exercise in logic, but also or rather an exercise in rhetoric? The object is to put your opponent in the wrong and yourself in the right, *in a socially acceptable manner*. (The significance of this qualification will become apparent shortly.)

1 *Straightforward or traditional ping-pong*

Here victory is achieved by demonstrating or assuming the untenability of pong, from which follows automatically the truth of ping (given the conventions of the game).

The *advantage* is that it gives you clear-cut victory with the minimum of fuss.

The *disadvantages* are:

(a) The nature of the game is rather obvious and your opponent may decline to play it.

(b) Unless your own position ('ping') is pretty invulnerable you are wide open to a counter-attack, whereby your opponent shows, by parity of reasoning, that '*not* ping, *therefore* pong', as we saw with Fletcher's attempt to establish situationism by refuting legalism. If, however, your position *is* invulnerable to counter-attack, why not simply *prove* ping in the first instance, and have done with it?

(c) The method looks (and is) distinctly polemical. Except in parts of the world where there is still no prejudice against polemics (*e.g.*, Germany, and possibly Scotland) you are liable to lose points by putting yourself into a position that is too blatantly superior.

2 *Transcending ping and pong*

This has the advantage of placing you virtually out of reach of attack by your opponent and thus making him feel thoroughly frustrated. He is beaten and he knows it. There is no doubt that, having transcended, you are in a more secure position than in (1).

However, there is a corresponding disadvantage. It is so exasperating to be transcended that sympathy is likely to go to your opponent. Your superiority is too bland for modern taste and you are likely to lose points for it.

3 *Ping and pong in dialectical tension*

This has the advantages of (2) without the disadvantages. You are in a superior position to the person who asserts ping, not realising that it has to be held in dialectical tension with pong, *and* to the person who asserts pong, without realising that it has to be held in dialectical tension with ping, *and* to the person who asserts both ping and pong, not realising that they have to be held in tension with one another. Yet you are so obviously, or at least apparently, doing justice to all of them that it would be thought most unreasonable of any of them to object to your proceedings.

Your position, then, is superior – and is, indeed, known to be superior – but it doesn't look blatantly superior. Moreover, holding ping and pong in dialectical tension is an uncomfortable posture (more uncomfortable than just asserting ping or pong), and this fact both cancels out any residual appearance of superiority and confers a further quite unchallengeable superiority where radical attitudes prevail. The chief disadvantage is that there is a very fine distinction between holding things in dialectical tension and just contradicting yourself.

4 *Identifying ping and pong*

This is extremely disconcerting to an opponent, because you have apparently given him all he wants – do you not affirm pong just as wholeheartedly as he does? – and yet the way you understand pong, *viz.* as, in the last analysis, indistinguishable from ping, seems to deprive it of the meaning he thought it had (which implied its *difference* from ping).

If he tries to come back into the game by protesting that pong is not simply reducible to ping, you challenge him to give a sense to pong which is not to be found in ping. Any suggestions he makes in reply you reject on the ground that they are not intelligible – the only criterion of intelligibility which you will permit being definability in terms of ping. This is the sort of manoeuvre – like selling a dummy in Rugby Football – which when coldly described sounds too elementary to take anyone in, but is amazingly effective in the heat of the game.

It only works, however, with an intelligent and suggestible opponent. A stubborn or unimaginative one is liable to maintain obstinately that he knows the difference between ping and pong, and there's an end on it. You couldn't have carried it off against Dr Johnson.

Concluding Comments

Before I finish I feel that in fairness to theological writers I ought to quote two examples of theologians themselves being wary of being drawn into the ping-pong game.

The first is from Gollwitzer's *The Existence of God as Confessed by Faith*, in which he exposes Herbert Braun's attempt to play it:

> Braun thinks in terms of the following alternatives: 'God as thinglike and given, and God as non-thinglike and not given'. To that there corresponds the antithesis: on the one hand the 'naive idea of God' that belongs to what is for us a 'vanished apocalyptic picture of the world', identical with a 'religious speculative assumption' which 'we cannot make in the world-view of today' – and on the other side 'we today'. Another corresponding antithesis is: 'theonomy as heteronomy' and 'theonomy as autonomy'. Another corresponding antithesis is: 'final salvation', as extension of the life of this world . . . and on the other hand

'final salvation fetched down from the heights of metaphysics' . . .[22]

Braun is obviously a good solid player in the German style.

The other example is from Bultmann, with whom we began. Here he is, in *Essays Philosophical and Theological*, refusing to be beguiled by the distinction between 'subjective' and 'objective':

> The demand that the interpreter must silence his subjectivity and extinguish his individuality in order to attain an objective knowledge is, therefore, the most absurd that can be imagined. It is sensible and right only in so far as we mean by it that the interpreter must silence his personal wishes with regard to the outcome of the interpretation . . . Otherwise the demand absolutely misjudges the nature of real comprehension. For the latter presupposes *the utmost liveliness of the comprehending subject, and the richest possible unfolding of his individuality.* Just as the interpretation of a work of poetry and of art can only be a success for those who allow themselves to be touched by it, so the comprehension of a political or sociological text can only be such for those who are stirred by the problems of political and social life.[23]

It will be apparent that my own attitude to the game of theological ping-pong is ambivalent. I recognise and hope I have succeeded in conveying to you something of the fascination of the game and the virtuosity with which it is played. But this very fascination, this very challenge to virtuosity, means that people are tempted to play it when they would be wiser not to, when a quiet walk along one or other of the everyday paths of reasonableness would be more rewarding, though less exciting. That is to say, theologians might first satisfy themselves (1) that there are only two possible alternatives; (2) that they cannot both be true or partly true. The fact is, I think, that theological ping-pong is a stimulating activity which can, however, become psychologically addictive. For theologians to forswear it utterly would be a sad impoverishment of life, but they ought not to let it become a habit.

12

THE PLACE OF SYMBOLS IN
CHRISTIANITY*

Professor J. L. Austin used to hold a seminar on Saturday mornings for philosophers younger than himself. Just after I had been elected to my fellowship at Keble I received a neatly written card from Austin asking if I would care to attend these Saturday mornings and adding that the topic for the term would be 'Marks, Symbols and Signs'. I arrived in Christ Church to find an assortment of my philosophical colleagues seated round a green baize table which was littered with maps, charts, plans, railway timetables and other exhibits. I remember vividly how proceedings opened. Austin leaned towards Jim Urmson, pointed towards one of the maps and said, 'Urmson, what would you say to me if I were to ask you, "Are there any symbols on that map?"?' There was a long pause at the end of which Urmson slowly shook his large, shaggy head and said, 'But I don't think you *would* ask me, "Are there any symbols on that map?"!'

I cannot remember how the discussion went after that, nor have I ever understood the full significance of this exchange. However, it does illustrate the caution associated with a certain philosophical approach. Austin would have been extremely unhappy with the broad generalisations that philosophical theologians have often made about the place of symbols in Christianity. Tillich, for example, held that all that we can know strictly about God is that he is *being* itself; beyond that we depend upon symbols which in some way participate in the power of being itself, much as a country's

* Originally read to a conference àt Chichester Cathedral, 1979.

flag participates in the power of the country whose flag it is.[1] Philosophical caution can be carried too far, but it is useful to start with some careful distinctions. Later on it may be appropriate to relax these and generalise more freely, as Tillich himself does, but it is all too common to hear words like metaphor, myth, simile, analogy, allegory, parable, symbol, image, model used in theological discussion as if they were entirely interchangeable.

A metaphor or simile is a figure of speech; a symbol or a model or an image may be expressed in language, but need not be. Myth, allegory and parable are all forms of narrative; whatever else they do, they tell a story. The story, like other examples of prose or poetry, may contain metaphors but is not itself a metaphor. Myths differ from parables or allegories in being essentially traditional. I can invent a parable or an allegory; I cannot invent a myth (the use of 'myth' in 'Plato's myths' is a specialised sense). Allegories differ from parables in the extent to which the elements in the story correspond to elements in the world which they are intended to represent. Symbols, models and images are all in a way representative, but symbols can be purely arbitrary or conventional, whereas models or images must bear some resemblance to what they represent. Models, typically, are *working* models; they may be simply scaled-down versions of the original, or, although in some respects different from it, they may have significant similarities of structure or function. Hence the use of 'models' in science. An image is, in the first instance, a visual representation which, unlike a diagram, shows how something looks, but it can be used in an extended sense to cover, for example, a 'mental image' which need not be visual. And it is also a generic term for figures of speech.

I have said nothing so far of analogy. An analogy is not, like a metaphor, a particular use of language, but a relationship of resemblance in some respect between one thing and another in virtue of which certain uses of language are possible. For example there is an analogy between following a path and following an argument in virtue of which the same word 'following' is appropriate. It would be odd, in this instance, to say that 'following' in 'following an argument' is metaphorical, or even ever was metaphorical. The use of the word 'follow' in its familiar sense is stretched quite naturally to cover the application to thinking.

After this preliminary sorting out, let us return to 'symbol'. In its more precise sense the role of symbols in Christianity would seem to be comparatively limited. There are symbols, but they do not have the importance Tillich ascribed to 'symbols' and they do not, as a rule, function as he said they do. The dove is a symbol of the Holy Spirit, the lion of St Mark; the fish is an early Christian symbol, but none of these is particularly indispensable nor is it obvious how any of them 'partakes in the power of that of which it is the symbol'. This is not surprising, since symbols can be purely conventional (although, strangely, Tillich gives a purely conventional symbol, *viz.* a national flag, as an illustration of the way in which a symbol partakes in the power of that which it symbolises). The fish as a Christian symbol is largely conventional and is thought to derive from the fact that the letters of the Greek word for fish can be taken as an acronym for Jesus Christ. There is a certain natural appropriateness in the dove symbol which reinforces and may have inspired its scriptural associations. And so on. You may be able to think of symbols, properly so-called, which illustrate Tillich's claim better, but I can think of only one.

For there is, undeniably, one symbol which is of central importance for Christianity – the cross. It is tempting to say that it is not conventional and not natural either but, rather, historical. The cross, as a symbol, has the significance it possesses for Christians because it represents Christ's crucifixion and, with it, all that it has meant for mankind. Thus it can symbolise suffering, redemption, self-sacrifice, triumph, according to the significance the crucifixion itself is given. Can we, in relation to it, make sense of Tillich's insistence on the participation of the symbol in that which it symbolises? We need first to distinguish between the innumerable particular instances of the cross symbol and the event of the crucifixion itself. The crucifixion itself can be regarded as not only the supreme instance of, *e.g.*, self-sacrifice, but also as the supreme symbol of self-sacrifice; and, as such, it does indeed partake of the virtue that it represents. By a natural extension we may say that the cross in the church or on the grave or by the wayside also partakes of this virtue. We do not in fact normally stop to make a distinction between the many crosses and the one cross. In somewhat the same way the V sign in the Second World War stood for Churchill, and Churchill both stood for and exemplified the will to victory.

A great deal more needs to be said about religious symbols, properly so-called. Some seem to be, in the first instance, natural symbols, like fire and water, bread and wine, light and darkness. In baptism and the Eucharist certain of these natural symbols are given a historical warrant through our Lord's institution and conventional recognition in the life of the Church. And the cross, too, can operate as a natural symbol independently of Christianity, signifying something like the point of intersection between time and eternity. But I am not competent to explore this topic,[2] and, in any case, I suspect that, when theologians like Tillich talk of symbols, they are not intending to restrict themselves to symbols narrowly conceived but have in mind the whole range of imaginative devices by means of which spiritual truth is communicated. The underlying conviction, which appears in Tillich's discussion, is that God and God's activity in the world cannot be straightforwardly or directly described or represented, but can only be suggested by comparison with familiar mundane things. This process of comparison is to be found less in the use of symbols, strictly so-called, than in the use of images, metaphors, parables and so on. If this is so, then a set of familiar problems arises which centre on the question how we can know that, in our thinking about God, we are applying these images, *etc.*, properly. Will the comparisons that worked in the past necessarily continue to work in the future? Can we invent entirely new ones or are we confined to looking for equivalents of the old?

These questions can be approached from two sides: the

philosophical or theological and the aesthetic. Although the two cannot be entirely separated, I think it is important that they should be distinguished. It could for instance be the case that the old symbols, as depicted in the art (including in this term the literature) of the past, can work perfectly well today for the communication of religious truth to our contemporaries but, for reasons that have nothing to do with religion but are specific to the present situation of the arts, a contemporary artist cannot make use of them. They may, for the time being, be played out aesthetically, although they are still effective religiously. No one can today write plays like Shakespeare, or design a Gothic cathedral, or – dare I say it? – compose a liturgy like Cranmer, yet this need not prevent those works of art from continuing to illuminate for us the fundamental mysteries of human existence.

However this may be, my present concern is with the philosophical or theological aspect of the problem. And I propose to take as my guide Austin Farrer in his Bampton Lectures *The Glass of Vision*.[3] Farrer uses the single word 'image' where Tillich uses 'symbol'. He argues that the thought of Christ himself was expressed in certain dominant images – the kingdom of God, the Son of Man, Israel, God as Father, God as Judge, God as Shepherd and so on. 'These tremendous images set forth the supernatural mystery which is the heart of the teaching.' 'The great images interpreted the events of Christ's ministry, death and resurrection, and the events interpreted the images: the interplay of the two is revelation.' The images had, for the most part, already appeared in the Old Testament and were to be further developed in the apostolic age.

In the apostolic mind the God-given images lived, not

statically, but with an inexpressible creative force. The several distinct images grew together into fresh unities, opened out into new detail and assimilated further image-material: all this within the life of a single generation. This is the way inspiration worked. The stuff of inspiration is living images.[4]

Farrer's description here calls to mind Livingstone-Lowe's account in *The Road to Xanadu*[5] of the workings of Coleridge's poetic imagination in *The Ancient Mariner* and *Kubla Khan*, and it is one of the strengths of his treatment that he is sensitive to the way inspiration works outside the domain of religion.

What you get when the images are combined, in the manner Farrer describes, and applied to the interpretation of events, is not just a picture but a story, and the peculiarity of the story lies in its capacity to weave together events that are straightforwardly historical with divine intentions and purposes which are not open in the same way to historical investigation. This is why it is not enough to say, as biblical theologians used to do, that God reveals himself in events. The events have to be interpreted before they become revelatory, and it is Farrer's claim that the interpretation is characteristically given in certain key images or symbols.

Farrer addresses his problem within the traditional framework of a distinction between natural and revealed theology, and he conceives of revelation in a strong sense as involving a process of supernatural inspiration. The images are to be thought of as divinely inspired. In this I should want to follow him, but it is not necessary to do so in order to appreciate the virtue of Farrer's treatment of inspiration or to recognise its difficulties. The questions which I mentioned earlier arise equally whether the images are divinely inspired in the way Farrer thought they were or whether they occur in the process of entirely human reflection, in particular the crucial question: How can we know that, in using them of God, we are applying them appropriately?

Farrer prefaced his book with the words of St Paul, 'For now we see through a glass darkly, but then face to face.' We need images because we cannot see God directly; not only can we not describe him in language that is adequate to the task, but we are not in a position to look away, as it were, from the partial picture we have painted (or which has been painted for us) so as to tell how far it falls short of a true likeness. But in that case surely we are left with nothing but a *via negativa*. We began with images as a second best, but now they seem to be no use at all. We could try to reassure ourselves with the thought that the images are authorised images – that God has in effect told us that we can trust them, but how can that help us if, in trying to think of God in any way, and of his 'speaking' to us, we are condemned to remain within the circle of images and never break through to the reality behind them?

At this point we can see the danger of using the one word, whether 'image' or 'symbol', to cover all the ways in which we try to conceive God. 'Image' is perhaps even more dangerous than 'symbol' at this point, because it tempts us to think in terms of the contrast between image (or picture) and original, and so to be puzzled as to how we can get at the original so as to compare the image with it. A symbol does not have to be like what it symbolises, and talking in terms of symbols may lead us to ask instead how the symbol can be used to help us grasp the thing symbolised without any thought of comparing image with original. The word 'model' is even better, because of its use in science. The physicist may employ a model of, for example, a uranium atom, but he does not judge the adequacy of his model by, as it were, looking at the uranium atom and then comparing the model with it. He tests and, if need be, modifies the model by undertaking experiments and seeing how well the model enables him to account for the data of observation. The use of the model is controlled by theory and both are controlled by observation. So may we not say that, in thinking about God, we do not rely on images or symbols alone, but interpret them and criticise them in the light of theism as a metaphysical theory? No doubt the traditional arguments for the existence of God do not, as was once supposed, operate as conclusive proofs of a deductive kind, but they do provide a good cumulative case for the belief that the world depends for its existence and its charac-ter upon a divine Creator. Introducing this 'philosophical theism' in his book *The Coherence of Theism*, Richard Swin-burne speaks of God as 'something like a "person without a body (i.e. a spirit) who is eternal, free, able to do anything, knows everything, is perfectly good, is the proper object of human worship and obedience, the creator and sustainer of the universe" ".[6] If by rational reflection we can arrive at such a concept of God and find reason to believe in his existence, we can go on to make sense of his communicating with us through images or symbols and we have some independent way of telling how these are to be understood and (within limits) how trustworthy they are. And, if that sounds altogether too abstract, we have also in our own experience some inkling of what is meant by the presence of God – enough to enable us to comprehend to some extent what we are told by saints and mystics whose experience is more continuous and profound than our own.

So when Farrer says, 'The veil, however impenetrable, is not blank. It is painted with the image of God, and God himself has painted it,'[7] we have a basis in reason and experience for believing that this is so.

But, it may be objected, this is so only if in our philosophical theism we really are independent of symbols or images. Would not a more careful look at natural or rational theology reveal that here too we are in no position to make statements about God that are literally true? Would not Tillich, for example, maintain that Swinburne's characterisation of God, for all its prosaic matter-of-factness, deals nevertheless in symbols? God is only 'something like' a person. He is free, but not just in the same sense or to the same degree as we are free; his power and his knowledge are not just like ours, and we have no experience of creation *ex nihilo*. So, he would say, these abstract-sounding concepts are themselves no more than symbols, suggesting comparisons that fall far short of the reality they purport to describe.

The force of this objection lies in the exhaustive and exclusive dichotomy it posits between 'literal' and 'metaphorical', so that, if we are persuaded that a usage is, in any sense, metaphorical, it cannot be literal. Any use of figurative language is then classed as 'metaphor', and all metaphors are assimilated to what we are inclined to call 'mere metaphors'. Thus 'the hand of the Lord' is clearly a metaphor, and, when we see a hand pointing down from the clouds on a Byzantine or Romanesque tympanum, we do not for one moment suppose (and nor did the original sculptors) that God really has a hand like that. It is merely a symbol. But what about knowledge or faithfulness or love as applied to God? Are they 'merely symbols' in a sense that would imply that 'God is all-knowing, or faithful or loving' is not the literal truth about God?

Bishop Berkeley distinguished between 'metaphorical' and 'proper' analogy. He says that by metaphorical analogy God is represented as having a finger or an eye, as angry or grieved: by proper analogy we must understand all those properties to belong to the deity which in themselves simply and as such denote perfection. Thus he concludes that it is a mistake to say we can never have any direct or proper notion of knowledge or wisdom as they are in the deity.[8]

'But', our objector will say in the spirit of Tillich, 'divine knowledge so transcends human knowledge – and it is human knowledge that provides the standard use of the word "know" – that at the very least we are compelled to concede that the meaning of the word has to be stretched to cover divine knowledge.' In this he is right; where he goes wrong is at the next stage, when he contrasts 'literal' with 'metaphorical', assimilates this stretched use of words to metaphor (*i.e.*, 'mere metaphor') and then concludes that what is asserted when the word 'know' is used in this stretched sense cannot be the literal truth. Consider, for example:

> The clever men at Oxford
> Know all that there is to be knowed
> But none of them knows half as much
> As intelligent Mr Toad.
> (Kenneth Grahame, *The Wind in the Willows*)

Surely we have no difficulty in understanding, if not in crediting, the omniscience of the clever men at Oxford. Whatever can be known, they know it.

A common objection to our being able to understand in the same way the concept of divine omniscience is that it involves 'extrapolating to infinity'. When we try to construct a scale of knowledge from the dog, say, by way of man to God, it always makes sense (if God's knowledge is infinite) to put something higher on the scale than anything that we have yet managed to conceive. But it is not clear that we are, in fact, in this sense, extrapolating to infinity. Mr Toad claimed that he knew more than twice as much as the clever men at Oxford, but he must have been wrong about this, as about so much else, if it is indeed the case that they 'know all that there is to be knowed'. Knowledge, as Berkeley insists, 'simply and as such denotes perfection'.

Of course, God knows in a way very different from the ways in which we men know. He does not need to infer from the observed to the unobserved; he is not exposed to the risk of error, and so forth. We cannot *imagine* what it is like for God to know. There are, moreover, well-known problems about the definition of omniscience. There is much about which we are bound to remain agnostic, but we can understand what is meant when, for example, it is said that we cannot deceive God, because he knows the secrets of all hearts. Similarly with love. Our human concept of love cannot be applied to God just as it is. It needs to be stretched; but in thinking of a love free from human limitations we are not venturing entirely into the unknown. Berkeley's insight is reflected in the language of familiar hymns: 'Love divine all loves excelling'; 'O perfect love all human thought transcending'.

By using certain words in stretched senses, by Berkeley's 'proper analogy' we can, then, achieve a framework of theistic theory by reference to which Farrer's 'grand images' can be understood and by which they can to some extent be controlled. In particular, Farrer's claim that 'divine truth is supernaturally communicated to men in an act of inspired thinking which falls into the shape of certain images'[9] need not itself be regarded as a metaphor that we are at a loss to interpret; for the language of 'speaking' or 'communicating' in this context is an instance of 'proper' rather than 'metaphorical analogy'. Of course, God does not speak as we do by modifying sound waves or writing on paper; yet we can suppose him to speak, if something – the words of the prophets, or the images that possess their minds, or the actions of Christ – can properly be read as conveying an intelligible message. There is the same sort of difference between 'he spoke by the prophets' and 'sermons in stones and books in the running brooks' as there is between 'speaking looks' and 'the breezes spoke to him of love'. The second figure in each pair is 'a mere metaphor' for the way in which nature arouses certain feelings in us; but when looks 'speak' and God 'speaks through the prophets', 'speak' is used in an extended sense and is not 'just a metaphor'.

What then of Farrer's 'grand images' themselves? Given this metaphysical framework they can illuminate God's relationship to his creatures – illuminate and not simply illustrate – because, like scientific models, they are capable of suggesting new insights, which can then be developed and tested by reason and experience. If God is our Father, he will hear our prayers and will care for all his children; if God is our Judge, we shall not escape judgement; if God is our Shepherd, he will bring us to safety.[10] As with scientific models, we have to distinguish those respects in which the analogy holds from those in which it does not. We are not tempted to infer, for example, that God has a wife or wears a wig, or that we are woolly, and this is not because we have no idea at all what God is like – if that were so, *all* our inferences would have to be negated equally – but because we have reason to ascribe to him as to ourselves attributes with which these implications are incompatible: he is one and is incorporeal. What impresses us about these 'grand images', by contrast with the concepts of rational theology, is their warmth and richness and resonance. Not only do they, as we have seen, enable us to grow in our understanding of God and his dealings with us, as the Christian tradition has continued to grow, but they have clear practical implications. If God is our Father, we should love one another; if he is our Judge, our own judgements can never be final; if God is our Shepherd we must learn to trust him. And there develops a complex reciprocal relationship between our conception of these human roles as applied parabolically to God and as we ourselves experience and assess them in their everyday context. Judges become more humane as they reflect that God is a merciful judge, and merciful judges in turn provide a better image for divine judgement. Or should do. The process can go wrong. The sort of reasoning it involves draws heavily upon personal judgement, itself formed by a reliable tradition.

The account I have sketched of the role of images or symbols in Christianity is liable to evoke criticism from two different quarters. On the one hand are those who would argue that the biblical tradition itself, with its full dramatic story, is all we need. The rest is an alien, philosophical importation. To this Austin Farrer himself provides the answer:

> To call God 'Father' and to say that He deals with us as sons is a parable; it asserts an analogy between what fathers do, and what God does. 'What God does' is outside the parable; it is that to which the parable is referred. And the phrase 'What God does' places God's action in the personal category; it is taken to be the same sort of phrase as 'What Henry does' and not at all the same sort of phrase as 'What prussic acid does'.[11]

That God is least misleadingly thought of as personal is a presupposition of the use of 'Father', 'Judge', 'Shepherd' in relation to him, and provides the essential link between these images (and others like them) and the creative activity of God. When, to use Farrer's expression, 'the parable' is referred to God, it is referred to a being who creates and sustains an ordered universe in which conscious agents are able to learn of his purposes and are free to co-operate with them. And this sort of 'doing', as Farrer insists, is not intelligible except in terms of personal agency. Without this essential reference, the biblical story is left hanging in the air.

The other, and opposite, criticism brings us back to Tillich. It is to the effect that justice has not been done to the utter transcendence of God, which is such that he cannot be captured by any of the categories of human thought. In endeavouring to provide, in however qualified a fashion, a framework of metaphysical theory within which the theologian can operate without prejudice to his proper concerns, all we have done is to add philosophical presumption to theological naiveté.

In the history of Christian thought, there have, not surprisingly, been marked changes of emphasis in relation to the use of images or symbols. Sometimes what has been stressed is their inadequacy, so that an entirely negative or mystical way is recommended. Sometimes these warnings are almost forgotten and the Christian imagination dwells with unquestioning confidence in the sacred story, with its rich profusion of images. Sometimes a refined and abstract rational theology has, with equal confidence, sought to dispense with the use of symbols entirely or to regard them as mere embellishments which assist the imagination but are not needed by the intellect. Throughout this history philosophy has played its part in shaping the dominant tradition of a particular period and in provoking reaction against it. The transcendence of God is a function of his holiness and, as such, is at the heart of Christian teaching. No philosophical theology can be adequate which denies it; but care has to be taken not to identify the transcendence of God, in the sense that is religiously important, with the way it has been interpreted within a particular philosophical system, whether it be the Platonism which so greatly influenced the formative period of Christian doctrine, or the Kantianism which, in one shape or another, underlies so much modern theology.

Philosophically speaking, I believe that we are in a better position now than for a very long time to maintain a proper balance between these two tendencies, the apophatic and the anthropomorphic. We are now much more aware of the essential part played by the imagination in all creative thought, not excluding natural science, and also of the mysteriousness of personal life. We have reason to believe that, through the controlled exercise of imagination, we can achieve a genuine, though always limited, understanding of the way things are, both in the world of nature and in the life of the mind. If, putting these two together, we seek to develop in our philosophical theology the personal categories which are, in any case, implicit in the Bible, we have to qualify them no doubt, as is typically the case also with scientific models – because only as qualified can they perform their explanatory role. But also the being we are led to posit in such a rational theology must, if the argument succeeds at all, be one that is transcendent in a unique sense, never to be fully comprehended. But this makes personal categories all the more appropriate, for we never know people so well that we could not know them better. We have here an image of divine inexhaustibility. Perhaps, then, to return to Tillich and to use his terminology, we do in this instance have a symbol which partakes in the virtue which it symbolises.

13

MAN – A REASONABLE BEING*

I wonder whether you were, to begin with, as puzzled as I was by the title of this lecture, given that it was to be the *first* lecture in a series on 'the Christian understanding of man'.

On the face of it, it looks much more suitable for the opening lecture in a series on 'the humanist understanding of man', or 'the rationalist understanding of man'. As this familiar use of the word 'rationalist' (= unbeliever) suggests, reason is often associated in people's minds with unbelief rather than with belief. Hence quite a lot of convinced Christians will have learned to be suspicious of 'reason'; and many uncommitted people who would like at any rate to find out about the Christian understanding of man are likely to assume that it will involve, at the least, some playing down of reason.

This will not necessarily discourage them, because distrust of reason is not confined to religious people, but is fairly widespread nowadays. (Hence 'rationalist' for 'unbeliever' has a faintly old-fashioned ring about it.)

All the same, I think on reflection that the instinct of those who planned the series was right and that we do need to concentrate at the start on 'man as a reasonable being'.

1. Let us, however, first give full weight to the suspicion that many people have about the place of reason in human life – not only in matters of religion but in relation to everything that is felt to be fundamental. There are two points I should like to make.

---

* Originally read as the first of a series of lectures entitled 'New Town Studies in Christian Theology', Bracknell, 1979.

(a) People distrust 'reason' in relation to religion because they regard it as superficial, unstable, deceptively clear. What you can be argued into you can be argued out of, and religion, they feel, should operate in the depths of a man's personality which mere arguments cannot reach. Theology itself as a rational discipline is an object of suspicion both to believers and to unbelievers, and for much the same reason, which was well expressed by F. H. Bradley in his celebrated remark about metaphysics: 'Metaphysics is the finding of bad reasons for what we believe upon instinct, but to find these reasons is no less an instinct.'[1] And this suspicion is intensified by the fact that people are not as a rule readily influenced by arguments when their deepest convictions are at stake. Hence the unsatisfactory nature of most television debates. The disputants tend so often simply to stumble past one another in the dark.

(b) I have spoken of 'deepest convictions', and these need not, of course, be religious. People's suspicion of reason, and their comparative imperviousness to argument, extends equally to their moral and political beliefs or their general philosophy of life. With respect to these also, most people take them over from their parents or their contemporaries; and when they react against the beliefs of their parents, as happens frequently in our own sort of society, they do not often rely on consciously and independently formulated arguments. Those who are liberated from tradition generally become slaves to fashion.

This is not at all surprising, nor is it wholly to be deplored. The complexity of the issues is such that few people, if any, can be expected to arrive at a set of reasoned convictions entirely from scratch. The best we can most of us hope to do is to draw upon some established set of ideas and treat them, so far as we are able, critically and reflectively. (Hence the absurdity of the sort of educational theory which aims to make children critical and creative without handing on to them anything substantial to be critical and creative about.) But having said this, in the endeavour to do justice to those who are suspicious of the search for reasons for belief in God (or anything else that matters to them), it is equally important to insist on the need for critical and reflective thought. It may not be necessary that everyone should subject his convictions to rational assessment and seek to articulate his reasons for believing whatever he does believe, but it is essential that some people should. If anyone doubts the dangers of uncritical enthusiasm or of ready acquiescence in prevailing attitudes, the recent television showing of *Holocaust* should provide a salutary reminder. There we saw conventionally good people led terribly astray. Indeed we need only look at any society or institution which restricts critical thought – *e.g.*, Poland or Iran as they are today. Society needs its intellectuals and the Church needs its theologians, though secular intellectuals and Christian theologians are alike in perpetual danger of silliness and superficiality, if they cease to be rooted in some solid tradition of thought and practice.

2. One explanation of this suspicion of reason is that we often have a very restricted conception of reason. Part of the problem about 'reason' is due to the difficulty of deciding what sort of reasoning is appropriate to the particular subject under discussion. The history of philosophy could be said to be the story of successive attempts to limit the concept of reason to some preferred type of reasoning, thus dismissing as beyond the scope of reason properly so-called any thinking that did not conform to the required definition. For many centuries deductive reasoning of the sort found in formal logic and mathematics was the preferred type. More recently it has been the sort of reasoning found in the natural sciences.

If the scope of 'reason' is narrowed in this way, it is naturally assumed that a great deal that matters in human life is outside the scope of reason altogether. Because it cannot be settled by science, any claim about the meaning and purpose of human life (whether religious or not) is thought not to be capable of being settled at all. The inevitable response to any such claim is 'You can't prove it.' So one of two things happens: *either* such concerns are abandoned altogether *or* they are thought of as matters of purely personal preference – of how the individual or the group chooses to think or feel.

My impression is that this narrowing of the scope of reason has affected our culture very profoundly, especially in our attitude to language. For if the language of science is the only accredited language, what is to be done with serious interpretations of human life (whether religious or not) which cannot be expressed in that language? Various responses are attempted; none of them, I think, satisfactorily.

(a) The first is simply to reject them as false because not scientific. There is evidence that quite a lot of children (especially boys) do this in early adolescence. They embrace a 'naive scientism'.

(b) The second is to adopt an approach to religion which is as like science as it can be made (given a rather naive understanding of science). Religious doctrines are regarded as cut-and-dried statements of quasi-scientific fact and the language of religion is interpreted in a flat, literalistic way. A conspicuous example of this is the 'creationism' which is currently being advocated in the United States as an alternative to Darwinian theories of evolution. But Christian fundamentalism is far from being the only example of this in our own society. The enormous vogue of astrology and of certain sorts of Eastern thought is due to its quasi-scientific character. It may be bogus science, but it has the flavour of real science – at least as it is popularly understood.

(c) The third is, as I have already said, to treat religion and everything to do with the meaning of life as 'entirely a matter of personal preference'. Its language is purely expressive or evocative and makes no claim to truth beyond 'It's true for me' or 'It's true for you.' People who respond like this have a deep repugnance against any attempt to seek clarity or consistency or coherence in their religious or other personal convictions, and regard rational criticism of them as wholly inappropriate.

All this (especially this last response) is doubtless related to what sociologists call the 'privatisation' of society. Increasingly the convictions which people expect to have in common are of a utilitarian kind, backed by common sense and scientific research. Everything else, religion included, is relegated to a private realm and regarded as a matter for purely private judgement.

But this attempt to narrow the scope of reason seems to me pretty clearly misguided in at least two ways:

(i) It is usually associated with an oversimplified idea of the nature of science itself.

(ii) In any case we are familiar with many examples of reasoning which are not scientific, but which we do and must rely upon.

I might, perhaps, add:

(iii) There is no sharp cut-off point between scientific and non-scientific reasoning. (These are, of course, matters of intense controversy among philosophers of science, and this itself is a fact of considerable significance. The common notion, that while the foundations of every other discipline are under constant threat those of science are unchallengeable, is simply mistaken. This does not mean, of course, that the claims of science as a form of knowledge cannot be satisfactorily vindicated; only that they are not, uniquely, beyond criticism.)

3. The most obvious examples of everyday reasoning which are not scientific have to do with our understanding of one another. Take the following exchange, from Jane Austen's *Emma*, between Emma and Mr John Knightley about Mr Elton's desire to please. Mr John Knightley is critical of this, but Emma defends Mr Elton:

'. . . There is such perfect good temper and good will in Mr Elton as one cannot but value.'

'Yes,' said Mr John Knightley presently, with some slyness, 'he seems to have a great deal of good-will towards *you*.'

'Me!' she replied with a smile of astonishment, 'are you imagining me to be Mr Elton's object?'

'Such an imagination has crossed me, I own, Emma; and if it never occurred to you before, you may as well take it into consideration now.'

'Mr Elton in love with me! – What an idea!'

'I do not say it is so; but you will do well to consider

whether it is so or not, and to regulate your behaviour accordingly. I think your manners to him encouraging. I speak as a friend, Emma. You had better look about you, and ascertain what you do, and what you mean to do.'

'I thank you; but I assure you you are quite mistaken. Mr Elton and I are very good friends, and nothing more;' and she walked on, amusing herself in the consideration of the blunders which often arise from a partial knowledge of circumstance, of the mistakes which people of high pretension to judgment are for ever falling into; and not very well pleased with her brother for imagining her blind and ignorant, and in want of counsel.[2]

We are not told by Jane Austen what, on either side, the reasoning processes are, but there is clearly reasoning involved here. Mr John Knightley and Emma are both trying to discern Mr Elton's motives and intentions. Notice that in such cases:

(a) It is possible to be right or wrong: the reader knows that in this case Mr John Knightley is right and Emma wrong.

(b) They are trying to explain Mr Elton's behaviour and are putting forward alternative theories or hypotheses: *i.e.*, generalised good-will or a partiality for Emma.

(c) It is a question of which hypothesis is best that accounts for the facts. No doubt either hypothesis could be squared with the evidence with a certain amount of special pleading – but the simpler and more coherent hypothesis is to be preferred.

(d) Sympathetic imagination is required in order to think up plausible theories as to Mr Elton's motives; and sound judgement is needed to decide which hypothesis accords best with the evidence. Since it is someone else's motives and intentions that are in question, there is need for 'empathy'; for the capacity to 'get inside' someone else's mind and see things as he sees them.

The delicate irony of the passage consists in Emma's self-deception: it is she who has 'high pretensions to judgment' which blind her to the true state of affairs.

Essentially the same sort of thinking as Emma and Mr John Knightley are doing here is done on a much larger scale by the historian when he is analysing the causes of a revolution or the rise of a political party. And here too it is important to rid the mind of bias; and the whole activity presupposes that this, although difficult, is possible.

We can see now why there is no possibility of making an entirely clear-cut distinction between scientific and non-scientific reasoning. For although the natural scientist has no need of empathy – he does not have to 'get inside' an electron and discern its intentions – the same is not true of the psychological and social sciences, which have human beings as their subject-matter.

(What I have just said is, of course, like anything one might say in this field, disputable. There is a running battle in the psychological and social sciences between those who believe that to be scientific they must deal entirely with what is 'objectively measurable', and those who do not.)

When we talk of man as a 'reasonable being' his capacity for this sort of thinking is what we chiefly have in mind. Men are able, subject to certain limitations, to stand aside from their immediate desires and interests and arrive at an understanding of the true state of affairs by a combination of imagination and judgement.

4. What are the limitations?

(a) First of all, in all thinking there is the constant danger of bias and self-deception (as in Emma's case), operating sometimes at a very profound level. The theories of Freud and Marx have alerted us in modern times to the irrational forces in human nature; how our thinking can be distorted by unconscious desires and conditioned by economic interests. Perhaps the eighteenth century was the only period in our history when there was anything like complete confidence in the powers of human reason – 'original sin' was of all orthodox doctrines the one that the Enlightenment most objected to.

But we need to maintain a balance here. Some Freudians and Marxists – and some theological exponents of original sin

– tend to overrun themselves to such an extent as to undercut their own theories. For if all our thinking is hopelessly biased or distorted, why should we accept the conclusions of Marx or Freud or Calvin?

(b) In any case, we can, at best, only approximate to the truth. Both in science and in religion we depend on metaphors or models which we have reason to believe represent the underlying reality up to a point – but only up to a point.

(c) Many philosophers in this century have held – and some still do – that among the limitations of human reason is an inability to answer, and even intelligibly to raise, questions about the meaning and purpose of the universe as a whole. We can seek to explain things in the world but not the existence and nature of the world itself. Questions about the meaning and purpose of human life are either to be answered by a decision on our part as to how we shall give our lives meaning; or they are not to be answered at all.

5. But if reasoning is what we have taken it to be, it is hard to see why its scope should be so drastically curtailed. To recapitulate, this sort of thinking (which we may call generally 'inductive' rather than 'deductive') is found, as we have seen, not only in science, but in history and other 'humane' disciplines. It is found even more obviously in our everyday dealings with people when we conjecture their motives and try to make sense of their actions. In all such cases we start with something which seems to require explanation and we cast around for some theory or hypothesis that might explain it. There are a number of things to notice about this.

(a) There is no recipe for hitting on good hypotheses. The capacity to do this is a large part of what makes the 'inspired' scientist or scholar. I believe the fashionable term is 'lateral thinking'.

(b) There will always be an indefinite number of hypotheses which are capable of explaining the facts; and any suggested explanation can be made to work, so long as enough complications are introduced. But the more complicated it is, the less satisfactory it is as an explanation.

(c) Hence the process of finding the best or most acceptable explanation is always a comparative one. And in the actual situation in which rival explanations are being canvassed, the parties to the debate are constantly, and wisely, modifying their positions to take account of criticisms directed against them by their opponents, and to do justice to newly discovered facts and newly confirmed theories.

This is not the occasion to consider in detail arguments for and against the existence of God. All that I want to suggest is that there is a recognisable pattern of argument. Theism – belief in God – is one among a number of possible world-views, each of which claims to make better sense of human experience than its rivals. The situation is rather like what we find when people are trying to make sense of a complicated and elusive set of clues, as when a jury is trying to reach a verdict, or a journalist is assessing a political situation, or a scholar is interpreting a text. Consider, for example, the problem of making sense of a passage of Plato. I am thinking not of translating it simply, but of understanding what Plato was trying to say. Notoriously scholars tend to disagree about such things. How do they seek to resolve their disagreements? It is exceedingly rare for one scholar to catch another out in a palpable mistake which proves him wrong at once. What usually happens is that each scholar relies on certain passages which seem to him (and, he would claim, to any reasonable person with the necessary scholarly equipment) entirely clear and which imply a particular theory as to what Plato was about. He challenges his opponent to make better sense of the whole thing. The opponent does not deny that the passages in question can at first sight be taken in the sense proposed by the other person, but argues that there are further passages – and, he maintains, more important ones – which conflict with this interpretation and favour another. It is up to him then, of course, to square the other person's passage with his own alternative interpretation of the whole thing. Each in this way builds up a cumulative case for his own interpretation. It isn't that one scholar has access to evidence which the other lacks; they both have access to all the evidence, *viz.*, what Plato wrote; and each is under an obligation to give some account of whatever evidence the other appeals to.

If one looks at the argument between theists and atheists with this comparison in mind, one finds, I suggest, a similar process going on. The theist claims that the existence of the world, and the very complex order that it manifests, call for an explanation and can be explained in terms of the creative activity of God. The atheist replies that explanation has to stop somewhere – there have to be some brute facts – and why not leave the existence of the world and its orderliness as primary unexplained data? Moreover, if everything has to be explained, God also has to be explained, so nothing has been gained by the theistic move. The theist replies that explanation should be carried as far as it can go, and that theism has a theoretical advantage in being able to explain more than atheism can. The process of explanation does not have to go on indefinitely, but only to the point at which no further gain in intelligibility is achieved. If we are looking for an explanation of the world, there is one at hand, namely God, but there is no further explanation then available which can, so to speak, improve on God.

At this stage of very abstract argument, we may say that the atheist's case has the advantage of economy – he can do without God; but the theist has the advantage of greater explanatory power. However, for all its abstract air, the cosmological argument does relate to an experience that is familiar to many people, what has sometimes been called 'cosmic awe' or 'cosmic wonder', the sense – very strong at some times and in some situations – that the world depends on something other than itself, which is aweful and mysterious.

So the argument between the theist and the atheist has to take account not only of the somewhat abstract considerations which come under the heading of the cosmological and teleological arguments, but also of the sense of the presence of God which saints and prophets have experienced and which comes under the heading of the argument from religious experience. Of course, it is not at all a simple matter to interpret such experiences which appear in such a rich variety of cultural forms, but they typically present themselves as a kind of direct awareness of a mysterious and impressive 'other' which cannot be identified with any thing or person in the natural world. Rudolf Otto in his *The Idea of the Holy* coined the word 'numinous' to express this experience of a 'mysterium tremendum et fascinans'.[3] Religious experience presents a problem both to the theist and to the atheist. The problem for the theist is to choose between the many different accounts in many different religions of the numinous. I have talked of the sense of the presence of God, and this is how Jews and Christians and Muslims would naturally talk; but Buddhists and Hindus would generally not interpret their experience as a personal encounter with God but rather as an absorption of their personality into a reality that is not conceived as personal. The problem for the atheist is to provide a convincing account of religious experience, and with it of the entire religious history of mankind, which will do justice to its character and effects. Such an account has to be a purely naturalistic one; it has to deny that these experiences are what they purport to be, *viz.*, instances of human awareness of the supernatural. And it is important to notice that the onus is upon the atheist to show reason why the experience is not to be trusted. Of course *no* experience is self-authenticating, but it is reasonable to accept claims made on the basis of experience unless sufficient reason is produced for not doing so. The obvious line for the critic to take in this case is that the experiences are illusory, and to trace the illusion to deep-seated fears and hopes. Thus Freud explained religion as a projection of the father figure, promoting an emotional substitute for the lost security of childhood; Marx as a compensation for political and economic oppression; Durkheim as a sort of collective representation of the majesty and otherness of society itself. These and other explanations have to be considered on their merits, but they face one obvious difficulty. Religion has been associated with the very highest human achievements in morality, philosophy and the arts, and the great religious figures have been men of outstanding intelligence and integrity. The more seriously one takes religion as what the atheist believes it to be, *viz*. a product of the creative human imagination, the more seriously one has to entertain the possibility that it is what the theist believes it to be, *viz*. not simply a product of the human imagination.

6. It seems pretty clear, in any case, that we have to put up with a good deal of uncertainty. Neither the theist nor the atheist is in a position to see more than in a glass darkly. Within this inevitable limitation each seeks to interpret in terms of his own basic position whatever is important to human life, although in the nature of the case neither interpretation is ever complete. Comparatively little that is important is totally unaffected by the choice that is made. For example the atheist views morality as essentially a human construction. It has an evident social utility, and human beings may frame ideals which go well beyond the requirements of social stability. But it is doubtful if morality can have for him the categorical character which it must have for the theist. For the atheist to do wrong is to offend against society or against specific persons. For the theist it is also to sin, to offend against God. The atheist regards human happiness as something to be realised as the result of his own efforts and those of other men, whereas the theist believes that happiness can ultimately be found only in God and that attempts to achieve it in entirely human terms will always fail. He will tend, then, not to be surprised if improvements in education and the abolition of poverty and injustice do not automatically make men happier. Least of all will he be surprised if men experience distress through their inability to find a meaning in life beyond what they as individuals or members of society choose to give it.

Wherever these differences of interpretation become apparent, they make their contribution to the total debate; and I think it is obvious that no clear-cut and easy answers are to be had. This does not mean, as is sometimes claimed, that it is all a matter of faith or existential commitment. It does mean that the issues are delicate, complex, profound and, although they have an intellectual structure, not to be understood without sensitivity, imagination and moral integrity.

7. In conclusion I must try to meet one obvious objection to what I have been saying about man as a reasonable being. I said at the beginning – if you remember – that it appeared at first to be an odd title for the first lecture in a series on the Christian understanding of man, and after all that I have said you may still find it odd. Surely you may feel religion (or at any rate Christianity) is a matter of faith and not of reason. The general tendency of my discussion has been to hold on to the conception of man as a reasonable being and to resist attempts to restrict the scope of human reason. But is this not a pagan rather than a Christian attitude, stressing the wisdom of man rather than the foolishness of God?

I think not. The typical pagan idea of reason was of a faculty ideally independent of the individual personality, capable of grasping eternal and immutable truths, a spark of the divine reason. Reason as I have been presenting it is a much more humble thing. It is a matter of individuals attempting, incompletely, to make sense of the total environment in which they find themselves and to respond rightly to it. It is an activity which involves the whole person and calls for sympathetic imagination, sensitivity and constant self-criticism. Man as a reasonable being is aware of his limitations and is concerned to relate himself to what lies beyond his individual personality, whether in the world of things or of persons. And mention of persons reminds us of two further things.

(a) It would be a very unreasonable man who thought he could work out for himself what other people thought and felt and intended (as perhaps Emma thought she could do with Mr Elton); and an even more unreasonable one who supposed that he could so work out the purposes and designs of God. We depend in both cases on what the other is willing to reveal to us.

(b) Reason can never in any case be just a matter of individuals working things out for themselves. No individual could conceivably think out for himself the entire content of any academic discipline or technical procedure, let alone of any religion or serious philosophy of life. The very process of making an original contribution to any of these presupposes a prolonged training in what has already been discovered and interpreted, in the course of which the individual has to take a great deal on authority. So reason must acknowledge the need for faith, and faith in its turn requires to be critically interpreted and appropriated.[4]

NOTES

1 The Layman's Predicament

1 Austin Farrer, *Interpretation and Belief* (London: SPCK, 1976), p. 162.
2 Kenneth Kirk, Bishop of Oxford 1937–54 and noted moral theologian. The remark may be apocryphal.
3 '"Logical Positivism and its Legacy." Dialogue with A. J. Ayer' in Bryan Magee, *Men of Ideas: Some Creators of Contemporary Philosophy* (Oxford: Oxford University Press, 1978), p. 107.
4 J. H. Plumb, source unknown.
5 Edmund Burke, *Reflections on the Revolution in France*, World Classics Edition of Burke's Writings, vol. iv (Oxford: Oxford University Press, 1928), p. 95.
6 Alain Peyrefitte, *Le Mal Français* (Paris: Plan, 1976), pp. 16–17.
7 R. G. Swinburne, *Faith and Reason* (Oxford: Oxford University Press, 1981), p. 54.
8 *ibid.*
9 W. K. Clifford, 'The Ethics of Belief' in *Lectures and Essays*, ed. Leslie Stephen and Frederick Pollock (London: Macmillan, 1886), p. 346.
10 William James, *The Will to Believe and Other Essays in Popular Philosophy*, Dover Edition (New York: Dover Publications, 1969), pp. 2–4.
11 John Henry Newman, *An Essay in Aid of a Grammar of Assent*, ed., with introduction and notes, Ian T. Ker (Oxford: Oxford University Press, 1985), p. 191.
12 Ludwig Wittgenstein, *On Certainty*, ed. G. E. M. Anscombe and G. H. von Wright; trans. Denis Paul and G. E. M. Anscombe (Oxford: Basil Blackwell, 1969), p. 234.
13 Newman, *Grammar of Assent*, p. 196.

2 Contemporary Challenges to Christian Apologetics

1 John Hick (ed.), *The Myth of God Incarnate* (London: SCM Press, 1977).
2 See Basil Mitchell, 'A Summing-up of the Colloquy: Myth of God Debate' in Michael Goulder (ed.), *Incarnation and Myth: The Debate Continued* (London: SCM Press, 1979), pp. 233–40.
3 See, for example, A. R. Peacocke, *Science and the Christian Experiment* (Oxford: Oxford University Press, 1971).
4 C. S. Lewis, *Miracles: A Preliminary Study* (London: Geoffrey Bles, 1947; London: Collins Fount Paperbacks, 1977).
5 See, for example, Thomas S. Kuhn, *The Structure of Scientific Revolutions*, Second Edition, Enlarged (Chicago: University of Chicago Press, 1970).
6 J. Bronowski, *The Ascent of Man* (London: BBC Publications, 1973).
7 Don Cupitt, *The Sea of Faith* (London: BBC Publications, 1984).
8 *Young People's Beliefs*, a research report by Bernice Martin and Ronald Pluck, prepared for the General Synod Board of Education, 1976, p. 47. They mention: P. Berger and L. Luckmann, *The Social Construction of Reality*, P. Berger, *The Social Reality of Religion*, and T. Luckmann, *The Invisible Religion*.
9 See, for example, James Barr, *Fundamentalism* (London: SCM Press, 1977).

3 Is There a Distinctive Christian Ethic?

1 C. S. Lewis, *The Abolition of Man* (Oxford: Oxford University Press; London: Geoffrey Bles, 1946; London: Collins Fount Paperbacks, 1978).
2 A. M. Macbeath, *Experiments in Living* (London: Macmillan, 1952), p. 369.
3 P. F. Strawson, 'Social Morality and Individual Ideal' in Ian T. Ramsey (ed.), *Christian Ethics and Contemporary Philosophy* (London: SCM Press, 1966), pp. 280–98.
4 Apropos the topic discussed in this essay, see also Basil Mitchell, *Morality: Religious and Secular. The Dilemma of the Traditional Conscience* (Oxford: Clarendon Press, 1980).

4 Should the Law be Christian?

1　Patrick Devlin, *The Enforcement of Morals* (Oxford: Oxford University Press, 1965), p. 9.
2　Basil Mitchell, *Morality: Religious and Secular. The Dilemma of the Traditional Conscience* (Oxford: Clarendon Press, 1980).
3　'Declaration on Religious Freedom' in *Documents of Vatican II*, ed. Walter M. Abbott, SJ (New York: Herder & Herder, 1966), ch. 1, para. 2, pp. 678–9.
4　*ibid.*, ch. 1, para. 3, p. 681.
5　Charles E. Curran, 'The Distinction Between the Moral and the Juridical Order', *Law and Justice* 82/3 (1984), p. 96.
6　*ibid.*, p. 98.
7　'Declaration on Religious Freedom', ch. 1, para. 7, p. 687.
8　Apropos the topic discussed in this essay, see also Basil Mitchell, *Law, Morality, and Religion in a Secular Society* (Oxford: Oxford University Press, 1970).

5 Thoughts on the Church and Politics

1　Paul Scott, *The Raj Quartet* (London: Pan Books, 1988).
2　Dennis Nineham, *The Use and Abuse of the Bible* (London: Macmillan, 1976), pp. 27f.
3　E. R. Norman, *Christianity and the World Order. BBC Reith Lectures 1978* (Oxford: Oxford University Press, 1979).
4　Herbert Butterfield, 'The Role of the Individual in History' in *Herbert Butterfield: Writings on Christianity and History*, ed. C. T. McIntire (New York: Oxford University Press, 1979), p. 23.

6 'Indoctrination'

1　Willis Moore, 'Indoctrination as a Normative Concept', *Studies in Philosophy of Education*, vol. iv, no. 4, p. 401.
2　Antony Flew, in reply to Moore, *Studies in Philosophy of Education*, vol. v, no. 2, p. 277.
3　Edmund Burke, *Reflections on the Revolution in France*, World Classics Edition of Burke's Writings, vol. iv (Oxford: Oxford University Press, 1928), p. 95. (Editors' Note: This is evidently a

favourite passage of Mitchell's. It appears also in 'The Layman's Predicament', p. 18, and in 'Neutrality and Commitment', p. 121. The present discussion is his fullest treatment of it.)
4 Aristotle, *Nicomachean Ethics*, 1103 A.33.
5 Gilbert Murray, *Euripides and his Age* (London: Thornton Butterworth, 1931), pp. 14–15.

7 Reason and Commitment in the Academic Vocation

1 Maurice Broady, in an earlier session of the conference.
2 T. S. Kuhn, 'Reflections on My Critics' in I. Lakatos and A. Musgrave (eds), *Criticism and the Growth of Knowledge* (Cambridge: Cambridge University Press, 1970), p. 262.
3 Plato, *Republic*, Book VI, 509d-end, Book VII, – 517c5, Everyman's Library Edition (London: J. M. Dent, 1935), pp. 204–10.
4 John Lucas, *Principles of Politics* (Oxford: Oxford University Press, 1966), p. 309.
5 *ibid.*

8 Neutrality and Commitment

1 Ian T. Ramsey, *Miracles: An Essay in Logical Mapwork*, Oxford Inaugural Lecture (Oxford: Clarendon Press, 1952).
2 P. F. Strawson, *The Bounds of Sense* (London: Methuen, 1966), p. 207.
3 René Descartes, *A Discourse on Method*, Everyman's Library Edition (London: J. M. Dent, 1912), p. 19.
4 *ibid.*
5 *ibid.*, p. 20.
6 Edmund Burke, *Reflections on the Revolution in France*, World Classics Edition of Burke's Writings, vol. iv (Oxford: Oxford University Press, 1928), p. 95.
7 Bertrand Russell, *The Autobiography of Bertrand Russell*, vol. 1 (London: George Allen & Unwin, 1967), p. 63.
8 David Hume, *A Treatise of Human Nature*, Part IV, Section VII, Everyman's Library Edition (London: J. M. Dent, 1911), pp. 253–4.
9 *ibid.*, p. 254.
10 *ibid.*

9 Faith and Reason: A False Antithesis?

1 See Thomas S. Kuhn, *The Structure of Scientific Revolutions*, Second Edition, Enlarged (Chicago: University of Chicago Press, 1970).
2 Michael Polanyi, *Knowing and Being* (London: Routledge & Kegan Paul, 1969), pp. 87–97.
3 H. H. Price, *Belief* (London: George Allen & Unwin, 1969), Lecture 9, *passim*.
4 B. F. Skinner, *Beyond Freedom and Dignity* (New York: Bantam Books, 1984).
5 R. S. Peters, *Ethics and Education* (London: George Allen & Unwin, 1966), p. 104.
6 Gilbert Murray, *Euripides and his Age* (London: Thornton Butterworth, 1931), pp. 14–15.

10 Philosophy and Theology

1 F. C. Copleston, *Philosophies and Cultures* (Oxford: Oxford University Press, 1980).
2 *ibid.*, p. 9.
3 See J. Hick (ed.), *The Myth of God Incarnate* (London: SCM Press, 1977), p. 202.
4 D. Z. Phillips, *Death and Immortality* (London: Macmillan, 1970), p. 50.
5 J. L. Mackie, *Ethics: Inventing Right and Wrong* (Harmondsworth: Penguin Books, 1977), pp. 46–8.
6 '"Logical Positivism and its Legacy." Dialogue with A. J. Ayer' in Bryan Magee, *Men of Ideas: Some Creators of Contemporary Philosophy* (Oxford: Oxford University Press, 1978), p. 107.

11 How to Play Theological Ping-Pong

1 Rudolf Bultmann, 'A Reply to the Theses of J. Schniewind' in Hans Werner Bartsch (ed.), *Kerygma and Myth: A Theological Debate*, trans. R. H. Fuller (London: SPCK, 1953), pp. 103–4.
2 Bultmann, 'Bultmann Replies to his Critics' in Bartsch (ed.), *Kerygma and Myth*, p. 201.
3 Bultmann, 'A Reply to the Theses of J. Schniewind' in Bartsch (ed.), *Kerygma and Myth*, p. 111.

4   H. Richard Niebuhr, *The Meaning of Revelation* (New York: Macmillan, 1960), p. 30.
5   *ibid.*
6   E. H. Gombrich, *Art and Illusion* (New York: Pantheon Books, 1960), p. 370.
7   Paul Tillich, *Theology of Culture* (New York: Oxford University Press, 1959), pp. 33–4.
8   Austin Farrer, 'An English Appreciation' in Bartsch (ed.), *Kerygma and Myth*, p. 219.
9   Joseph Fletcher, *Situation Ethics* (Philadelphia: Westminster Press, 1966), p. 55.
10 Tillich, *Theology of Culture*, pp. 4–5.
11 *ibid.*, pp. 7–8.
12 Reinhold Niebuhr, *The Nature and Destiny of Man*, vol. 1 (London: Nisbet, 1941), p. 279.
13 *ibid.*, p. 278.
14 *ibid.*, pp. 279–80.
15 W. G. Maclagan, *The Theological Frontier of Ethics* (London: George Allen & Unwin, 1961), p. 113.
16 *ibid.*, p. 157.
17 *ibid.*, p. 164.
18 John Baillie, *The Sense of the Presence of God* (New York: Scribner's, 1962), p. 64.
19 Ian T. Ramsey, *Religious Language: An Empirical Placing of Theological Phrases* (London: SCM Press, 1957), p. 183.
20 *ibid.*
21 *ibid.*, pp. 183–4.
22 Helmut Gollwitzer, *The Existence of God as Confessed by Faith*, trans. James W. Leitch (London: SCM Press, 1965), pp. 82–3.
23 Rudolf Bultmann, *Essays Philosophical and Theological*, trans. James C. G. Greig (London: SCM Press, 1955), pp. 255–6.

12 The Place of Symbols in Christianity

1   Paul Tillich, *Myth and Symbol*, ed. F. W. Dillistone (London: SPCK, 1966), p. 17.
2   The subject of natural and conventional symbols is explored by Sir Ernst Gombrich, *Meditations on a Holy House* (London: Phaidon Press, 1963), pp. 14ff.

3 Austin Farrer, *The Glass of Vision* (London: Dacre Press, 1948).
4 *ibid.*, pp. 42ff.
5 J. Livingstone-Lowe, *The Road to Xanadu* (London: Constable, 1927).
6 Richard Swinburne, *The Coherence of Theism* (Oxford: Oxford University Press, 1977), p. 1.
7 Farrer, *Glass of Vision*, p. 61.
8 George Berkeley, *Alciphron*, Fourth Dialogue, in A. A. Luce and T. E. Jessup (eds), *Works of George Berkeley* (London: Nelson, 1950).
9 Farrer, *Glass of Vision*, p. 57.
10 See Janet Martin Soskice, *Metaphor and Religious Language* (Oxford: Clarendon Press, 1985), p. 112.
11 Austin Farrer, 'Revelation' in Basil Mitchell (ed.), *Faith and Logic: Oxford Essays in Philosophical Theology* (London: George Allen & Unwin, 1957), p. 95.

13 Man – A Reasonable Being

1 F. H. Bradley, *Appearance and Reality* (London: George Allen & Unwin, 1916), Preface, p. xiv.
2 Jane Austen, *Emma*, ed. and introduced Ronald Blythe (Harmondsworth: Penguin Books, 1966), pp. 133–4.
3 Rudolf Otto, *The Idea of the Holy*, trans. John W. Harvey (Oxford: Oxford University Press, 1950), pp. 5–40.
4 Apropos the topic discussed in this essay, see also Basil Mitchell, *The Justification of Religious Belief* (New York: Oxford University Press, 1981).

The C. S. Lewis Centre

The C. S. Lewis Centre for the Study of Religion and Modernity is a Christian research organisation working in partnership with Hodder and Stoughton to publish thought-provoking material concerning the relationship between the Christian faith and the modern world. Following C. S. Lewis' example, it is the Centre's policy to reach a broad market, speaking to 'everyman' in an intelligent and informed way, and responding to the challenge presented to orthodox belief by the secular culture of our contemporary society.

Edited by Dr Andrew Walker
and Dr James Patrick

A CHRISTIAN FOR ALL CHRISTIANS

Essays in honour of C.S. Lewis

A CHRISTIAN FOR ALL CHRISTIANS has three purposes. Firstly, to look at those influences and friendships that helped form the 'real' Clive Staples Lewis. Secondly, to examine the reasons for his enduring popularity with virtually all shades of Christians by examining the true meaning of his teaching and faith. And finally, to provide a complete list of biographies and bibliography of works by and about C.S. Lewis.

Subjects include:

THE CHRISTIAN INFLUENCE OF
  G.K. CHESTERTON by Aidan Mackey
C.S. LEWIS AND IDEALISM by James Patrick
'LOOK OUT! IT'S ALIVE!' C.S. LEWIS
  ON DOCTRINE by Jacques Sys
C.S. LEWIS THE MYTH-MAKER by Paul S. Fiddes
HOW TO SAVE WESTERN CIVILISATION:
  C.S. LEWIS AS PROPHET by Peter Kreeft
DID C.S. LEWIS LOSE HIS FAITH?
  by Richard L. Purtill

Dr William Abraham

THE LOGIC OF EVANGELISM

There is a rift today between evangelism and theology. As C. S. Lewis commented, "We need two sorts of evangelists: evangelists for the head and evangelists for the heart". William Abraham points out that we are not short of the latter, and innovates in providing the much needed academic and theological undergirding of evangelism so often absent today. Yet he is the first to assert that evangelism is one-sided if it is perceived only as a proclamation of the Gospel: attendance at a Billy Graham rally can only be the first step. The real work of evangelism happens after a commitment is made.

William Abraham tells us that evangelism is an ongoing, life-long process of understanding and growth, starting with the message of the Gospel and its proclamation. It continues with the full and proper initiation of the new convert into a local church through baptism and a change in lifestyle dictated by the desire to conform to a new, Christian morality, and through an understanding and personal appropriation of the Creed, the spiritual gifts, and of the spiritual disciplines. Evangelism finds its true fulfilment in the now-established convert's commitment to further evangelisation.

Edited by Andrew Walker

DIFFERENT GOSPELS

DIFFERENT GOSPELS identifies the undermining of the apostolic faith by the relativism, subjectivism and the rationalism of 'modernist' thinkers and theologians. The book is split into three main sections. It begins with interviews with four renowned elder statesmen from four different churches, who reflect on the state of the Church in the modern world.

The second and main section analyses modernist theories and methodologies and provides a vigorous defence of the doctrines of the Trinity, Incarnation and Resurrection, as well as defending the reliability of the historical basis of the New Testament and affirming the reality of miracles.

The final section discusses the relationship between the Christian faith, freedom and modernity, and asserts that the threat to the Christian faith comes not only from theological 'modernism', but also from the materialistic, individualistic nature of modern life.

DIFFERENT GOSPELS contains interviews with Lesslie Newbigin, Metropolitan Anthony, Cardinal Suenens and Professor Tom Torrance, and contributions by Alister McGrath, Thomas Smail, Peter Toon, Gavin D'Costa and Andrew Walker.

Andrew Walker

ENEMY TERRITORY

The reality of the Devil is denied in many of today's churches. Yet Christians need to see the problems of the modern world within the context of the Great Battle: the spiritual warfare between the forces of good and evil, of God and the Devil. Adapting a central metaphor from C. S. Lewis' famous Broadcast Talks in 1942, Andrew Walker insists that Christians need to see the world as enemy-occupied territory which, under Christ's command, they need to liberate for God.

To be effective in battle, however, it is crucial to know the enemy. In the main section of the book, the author identifies certain features of modernity as the Devil's deadly strategy against humanity and the Church: modernist ideologies in theology, science and morality, and the social and cultural changes that have accompanied modern industrialisation.

Andrew Walker goes on to outline methods of resistance and counter-attack in the Christian struggle for the modern world. He lays particular emphasis on overcoming intellectual laziness in the fight against modernism, working together in unity, applying spiritual disciplines such as prayer and fasting, and he underlines the need to provide a theological framework for social and political action.

Finally, he claims that the liberation of enemy territory is nothing less than the transfiguration of the world by God's kingdom of love.